Not Only English

Not Only English

Affirming America's
Multilingual Heritage

Edited by

Harvey A. Daniels
National-Louis University

National Council of Teachers of English
1111 Kenyon Road, Urbana, Illinois 61801

Staff Editor: Robert A. Heister

Cover Design: Michael J. Getz

Interior Book Design: Tom Kovacs for TGK Design

NCTE Stock Number 33630-3020

Library of Congress Cataloging-in-Publication Data

Not Only English : affirming America's multilingual heritage / edited by Harvey A. Daniels.
    p.   cm.
    ISBN 0-8141-3363-0
    1. Language policy—United States. 2. English language—United States—Political aspects. I. Daniels, Harvey, 1947-
P119.32.U6N68   1989
306.4'4973—dc20   90-31354
                                        CIP

Contents

Preface

Although many Americans assume that English is the official language of the United States, it is not. That is to say, nowhere in the U.S. Constitution is English privileged over other languages, and no subsequent federal law establishes English as the language of the land. And yet we are historically, culturally, unanimously, and without question an English-speaking country. Our legislatures, courts, schools, and most other institutions go about their daily business as if English were indeed the official national tongue.

To fill what they perceive to be a legal gap, several states have recently made or contemplated laws to make English their official language: either ceremonial laws to give English the same status as the state bird, or flower, or fossil, or exclusive ones that specifically prohibit the use of languages other than English in certain contexts. Over the past few years, this drive to officialize English has grown into a widespread popular movement, stirring up noisy and fractious debate. Several sophisticated, well-financed national lobbying groups continue to press for further state legislation as well as for a federal constitutional amendment to "legally protect" the English language.

The National Council of Teachers of English (NCTE) has taken a special interest in this growing national issue. As people professionally concerned both with the English language and with the education of young people, many NCTE members have been deeply worried by the aims and tactics of the language protection movement, as well as its potential consequences for our students. This concern was strongly expressed in a unanimous resolution passed at the Council's 1987 Annual Convention:

> RESOLVED, that the National Council of Teachers of English condemn any attempts to render invisible the native languages of any Americans or to deprive English of the rich influences of the languages and cultures of any of the peoples of America;
>
> that the NCTE urge legislators and other public officials to oppose any action intended to mandate or declare English as an official language or to "preserve," "purify," or "enhance" the language. Any such action will not only stunt the vitality of the language,

but also ensure its erosion and in effect create hostility toward English, making it more difficult to teach and learn;

and that the NCTE widely publish this resolution to its affiliates and other professional organizations through news releases, letters to legislators, board of education and other state officials, especially in those states attempting to legislate English as an official language.

During the same year, the NCTE also signed on as a charter member a group called English Plus, a coalition of thirty cultural, labor, and educational organizations joined to oppose the English-only movement and to operate the English Plus Information Clearinghouse (EPIC).

Many people outside the profession—and some on the inside—were surprised to hear that English teachers, of all people, would oppose the apparent uplifting of their own professional specialty. Self-interest, if not principle, seemed to favor NCTE's strong endorsement of English-only legislation. But as this book will explain, official-English policies hold grave dangers for teachers and students of English, as well as for many other Americans.

The charge for this book came from the NCTE's Commission on Language, the standing committee responsible for monitoring the English-only movement and making recommendations to the larger Council. Under recent chairpersons James Stalker and Jesse Perry, commission members spent considerable time tracking and studying the movement. In 1988, following the passage of English-only legislation in Colorado, Arizona, and Florida, the Commission urged that the Council do more to oppose language protectionism. Specifically, the Commission suggested that a book be prepared that would explain the Council's position to both members and outsiders, and provide the kinds of historical, linguistic, and educational background necessary to understand and combat language restrictionism.

With these goals in mind, twelve outstanding scholars and educators, all of whom have played central roles in recent language policy debates, were asked to contribute chapters. Instead of assigning narrow subtopics, the editor asked the authors to focus upon whatever aspect of the controversy most closely intersected with their own research interests, or touched their hearts, or both.

The result is a book in four sections. The first four chapters describe the nature, development, and extent of the contemporary English-only movement. Harvey Daniels, Dennis Baron, Elizabeth Frick, and Elliot Judd ground the current controversy in its deep historical context, and show how strikingly today's crisis parallels prior debates. Professor Baron also contributed important language and ideas to this preface. In the second section, Roseann Gonzalez and James Stalker look at the potential impact of the proposed federal English Language Amendment, both upon the public at large and the English teaching profession. Next, Vivian Davis, Victor Villanueva, and James Sledd analyze the causes and motivations of language protectionism, uncovering sources which range from general cultural turmoil to plain racism. And finally, Mary Carol Combs, Lynn Lynch, Geneva Smitherman, and Harvey Daniels suggest political and professional responses to the English-only movement, concluding with practical ideas for individual teacher-citizens who want to work for linguistic pluralism.

Most people who have studied today's English-only movement are struck by its remarkable similarity to past controversies, by the way it reenacts America's recurrent intolerance of ethnic minorities and immigrants. There is no doubt that this era will ultimately be looked back upon as another cycle of bigotry disguised as a debate about language. In hindsight, the underlying meaning of today's events will be perfectly clear, and people looking back may well ask: Couldn't those people see what was behind the English-only movement? Who voted for all those English-only laws? Why wasn't there a more effective, widespread opposition? And was this kind of discrimination socially acceptable in the 1990s?

The goal of this book is to make that interval unnecessary; to help us find, right now, the balanced perspective which hindsight also provides, but without waiting for years while acting out a destructive, unexamined pattern.

For all of us, this means reviewing some history, learning a bit of linguistics, and critically interpreting the claims of the different sides in the debate. For teachers, there are special, additional duties. We must not only fulfill our personal responsibility as thoughtful, independent citizens, we must also interpret these language issues for students, parents, and school communities. This book is intended to help teachers of English, language arts, and other school subjects comfortably take on that difficult role. The authors also hope that this book will help other interested citizens to sort out the issues for themselves.

I The Nature and Origins of the English-Only Movement

1 The Roots of Language Protectionism

Harvey A. Daniels
National-Louis University

The United States has always been a multilingual country. The history of the American people, the story of the peoples native to this continent and of those who immigrated here from every corner of the world, is told in the rich accents of Cherokee, Spanish, German, Dutch, Yiddish, French, Menomonie, Japanese, Norwegian, Arabic, Aleut, Polish, Navajo, Thai, Portuguese, Caribbean creoles, and scores of other tongues. Of all the richnesses that define the complex culture of this nation, none is more sparkling, more fascinating, or more evocative of our diverse origins than our plural heritage of languages.

Through much of our history, Americans have viewed this linguistic diversity as either a blessing or a simple fact of life. The founding fathers carefully omitted any constitutional provision establishing an official language—indeed, many of the founders were German-English bilinguals themselves. From the earliest days of nationhood, through both law and custom, the use of various languages other than English has been officially sanctioned in education, government, and commerce. The public and private use of a variety of languages has usually been treated as business-as-usual in a nation of immigrants.

But as Americans, we have also shared and treasured English, by custom and practice, and without challenge, as our common national language. While we trace our origins among peoples of many languages, we have always had our strong lingua franca. Indeed, America has developed one of the most efficient patterns of linguistic assimilation in the world. For more than two centuries, non-English speakers arriving in America typically have moved from their native language, through a bilingual stage, to monolingual English-speaking within three generations—and among some of today's immigrants, the process is occurring in only two generations (Veltman 1988).

The predominance and civic necessity of English is unquestioned in America; indeed, few countries in the world enjoy such a well-

3

established, stable national language standard. For just one contemporary example of this acceptance: among a sample of contemporary Hispanic immigrants, 98 percent believe their children must learn to speak English "perfectly" in order to succeed—compared with 94 percent of Anglos holding the same opinion (Crawford 1989, 60). Of course, we Americans have also had our share of sociolinguistic conflicts, and as this book will explain, the most painful of these have occurred in the past seventy-five years. But still, the overwhelming fact of our national linguistic life has been the predominance of English and its remarkably quick mastery by new Americans.

Given this broad historic picture of linguistic stability and cultural consensus, then, it is somewhat surprising to find that language differences have become a searing political issue in the 1990s. Today, several powerful national lobbying groups are calling for the passage of both state and federal laws to officialize English, for cutbacks in bilingual education programs, and for a host of other legal measures designed to "legally protect" the common language. These groups argue that America is in a profound cultural crisis, that the very dominance of English is suddenly in peril, and that only concerted national legal action can save its central role in our culture. To these people, the image of Babel, a country confounded by a multiplicity of languages, is not just a Biblical parable but an unfolding American reality.

According to U.S. English and other groups, the old pattern of language shift is no longer working; today's immigrants are different, and they are not assimilating like the Germans, Swedes, Poles, and Italians once did. Hispanics in particular are accused of actually *refusing* to learn English, instead demanding separate government-funded services delivered in their native language right to their ethnic neighborhoods. This new crop of immigrants, as one leader of the official-English movement explains, prefers to hide in ethnic ghettos, "living off welfare and costing working Americans millions of tax dollars every year" (Horn, 1).

The American public has been stirred by such accusations. How dare immigrants withhold this minimal act of allegiance—of plain simple respect—refusing to learn the common language of their adopted homeland? One need not be an ultrapatriot to be offended by such apparent intransigence and ingratitude. Nor has it been difficult for protectionist groups to spin frightening propaganda out of contemporary headlines. "I'm furious, and I'm scared," begins a solicitation letter from the director of El-Pac, the political lobbying arm of U.S. English. "I'm furious that the presidential nominee of a major American political party delivered a large portion of his acceptance speech *in a foreign language.* . . . Dukakis crossed a line that has never been crossed before. He signaled to all Americans that, in his search for Hispanic votes, he is willing to *embrace a new way of life* for us all—official bilingualism" (Zall, 1).

Their fears stoked by such appeals, thousands of good-hearted, patriotic, loyal Americans—often consciously honoring their own immigrant ancestry—have voted in large majorities to support official-English referenda recently appearing on the ballot in many states. By now, sixteen states have passed some version of an official-English law, and many more are considering such legislation. These states and the dates of their legislation are listed below:

Arizona	1988
Arkansas	1987
California	1986
Colorado	1988
Georgia	1986
Florida	1988
Illinois	1969
Indiana	1984
Kentucky	1984
Mississippi	1987
Nebraska	1923
North Carolina	1987
North Dakota	1987
South Carolina	1987
Tennessee	1984
Virginia	1981

*Hawaii and Louisiana have laws which give legal status to multiple languages.

What have been the outcomes of these state official-English statutes? The laws passed in the last few years have had a largely symbolic impact thus far. But from each of the new official-English states come reports of uncivil confrontations: in Colorado, a bus driver orders Hispanic children to stop speaking Spanish on the way to school ("English Only," 1989, 6); in Denver a restaurant worker is fired for translating the menu for a Hispanic customer (EPIC, March/April, 1988); in Texas, Spanish-language radio stations are the subject of FCC petitions (Bikales 1985); in Coral Gables, Florida, a supermarket checker is suspended without pay for speaking Spanish on the job (Gavin 1988);

in Huntington Beach, California, court translators are forbidden to use Spanish in personal conversations (EPIC, March/April, 1988).

Still, large-scale official changes have not yet occurred in most areas. Few public officials—especially elected ones—have been eager to enforce English-only laws, especially when doing so would effectively terminate a previously available public service, and some, like the mayors of Denver and San Antonio have been outwardly defiant. And courts have struck down some English-only rulings, such as the Huntington Beach translators' case noted above. But, always keeping up the pressure, U.S. English and other groups continue to file specific challenges to particular practices, and these will gradually work their way through the legal system. It is not yet clear how the courts will rule, especially when language issues conflict with civil rights, a collision which is bound to occur frequently in these disputes.

What are some of the uses of non-English languages that U.S. English and others will try to terminate under the new statutes? Below are listed some practices and situations already targeted for abolition by U.S. English in one or more states:

- translators in public hospitals
- 911 emergency service
- voting materials, instructions, and ballots
- court reporters and other legal services
- bilingual education in public schools
- school materials, parent conferences, report cards
- driver's license regulations and examinations
- non-English radio and television broadcasting
- non-English holdings in public libraries
- street signs, park names, commemorative naming of public sites
- directory assistance
- telephone books and yellow pages
- tourist information
- public housing listings and information
- bus and train schedules and signs
- general advertising, business signs, billboards, menus (Zall; Crawford 1989; *EPIC Events*, 1988, both issues)

This list is a reminder, perhaps, of the degree to which public and private services already are routinely provided in non-English languages throughout America, in many cases to ensure public safety or simple justice.

As the list also suggests, U.S. English will probably not be satisfied when all immigrants learn English—they seem also to want all public reminders of the existence of other languages removed from America. They do not want to have to hear any Spanish in public, see any billboards, flip past any TV channels in languages other than English. Indeed, many U.S. English documents describe it as a violation of English speakers' civil rights to hear "foreign" languages in the street, to be made to feel a stranger in one's own country.

And as the above list further demonstrates, some English-only adherents feel that death is not too severe a penalty for an immigrant's failure to speak English. The denial of translator services in hospitals is one of the most telling planks in the official-English platform. The Florida director of U.S. English has specifically called not just for the termination of the 17 employees who translate between doctors and Spanish-speaking patients at Dade County's Jackson Memorial County Hospital, but also for elimination of prenatal, postnatal, and postsurgical materials and conferences in non-English languages (Robbins 1985). U.S. English is willing, in other words, to risk the lives of fellow Americans in the name of its language standards. As one U.S. English leader declared, just before going off to run for Congress from a Florida district, people who cannot explain a fire location or an ongoing crime in English have no right to police and fire protection through the 911 emergency number ("Florida English," 1986).

U.S. English holds an analogous view of education. Adherents essentially insist that being schooled immediately and exclusively in English is more important than achieving literacy or learning subject matter. Never mind that such an approach violates the best-proven educational practices and guarantees unnecessary academic failure for many youngsters. As one widely distributed U.S. English promotional piece puts it, "If our society can't afford some scholastic failure, then we can't afford immigration" ("Frequently Used Arguments," U.S. English). U.S. English proponents describe it as unrealistic and unattainable for immigrant children to succeed in school at the same rate as American-born children. Accordingly, U.S. English and the other language restrictionist groups oppose bilingual education, which has been amply shown to be the most educationally effective and socially benevolent approach to the education of non-English-speaking students.

For the time being, the national English-only lobby seems only modestly interested in enforcing its newly passed state laws. Instead, the movement's main energies are devoted to passing similar laws in additional states and attacking federal bilingual education policy. The overall strategy seems to be to get some official-English law on the books of a majority of states and to continually fan public resentment over schooling policies that "degrade English" and "cater" to immigrants. These activities seem aimed to develop momentum behind the English Language Amendment, the proposed federal constitutional amendment which has been stalled in committee for years, lacking the broad sponsorship that might coalesce if a snowballing public sentiment can be created.

Language Debates in the Twentieth Century

There has probably been more discord about language differences in America during the last seventy-five years than there was between Plymouth Rock and the turn of this century. A very distinct watershed occurred between 1915–20, when differences in language became a very contentious public issue. Emblematic of the period, Theodore Roosevelt asserted in 1919: "We have room for but one language here and that is the English language, for we intend to see that the crucible turns out people as Americans and not as dwellers in a polyglot boarding-house" (Crawford 1989, 23).

The increased concern with language differences was obviously related to the imminent World War, but it was also concurrent with a major shift in the quantity and type of immigration to the United States. After a steady flow of northern Europeans in the nineteenth century, there now appeared a growing number of southern and eastern European immigrants (members of the "Mediterranean" and "Alpine" races, according to the eugenicists of the day)—Italians, Poles, and Jews of various nationalities. This new type of immigrant was viewed darkly by many American politicians and educators, and thought to suffer from high levels of feeble-mindedness, disloyalty, Popery, and other shortcomings. In one of the more popular books of the day, Charles Benedict Davenport warned that

> the population of the United States will, on account of the great influx of blood from South-eastern Europe, rapidly become darker in pigmentation, smaller in stature, more mercurial, more attached to music and art, more given to crimes of larceny, kidnapping, assault, murder, rape, and sex-immorality . . . [and] the ratio of insanity in the population will rapidly increase. (Davenport 1911, 219)

Davenport was especially worried about the "hordes of Jews" arriving from southeastern Europe. According to Davenport, Jews, with their

> connection with prostitution . . . and intense individualism and
> ideals of gain at the cost of any interest, represent the opposite
> extreme from the early English and more recent Scandinavian
> immigration with their ideals of community life in the open coun-
> try, advancement by the sweat of their brow, and the uprearing of
> their families in the fear of God and the love of country. (1911, 219)

During this period there were vociferous debates over how—and
whether—persons so alien to the American "Nordic" race could assimilate. There was a vocal national concern that these immigrants
were simply not of the quality and character of English or Scandinavian stock. While Germans were still viewed as genetically superior to
Mediterranean types, the outbreak of war made the Germans the most
despised people of all. The German accent was virtually eradicated
from public use in America within a few years. In 1915, 24 percent of
American high school students were studying German; by 1922 only 1
percent were doing so. Indeed, this period of linguistic intolerance
caused a catastrophic drop in enrollments in *all* foreign languages from
which our educational system has never recovered (Crawford 1989,
24).

Around this time, the fledgling National Council of Teachers of
English, in its first decade of existence, hopped on the protectionist
bandwagon by cosponsoring a national event called "Better Speech
Week." In schools throughout America, students were enlisted in
"Ain't-less," "Final-G," and other assorted grammatical tag-days designed to heighten linguistic vigilance. The centerpiece of this annual
festival, which ran for more than a decade, was the following pledge,
recited by schoolchildren all around the country:

> I love the United States of America. I love my country's flag. I love
> my country's language. I promise:
> 1. That I will not dishonor my country's speech by leaving off the
>   last syllable of words.
> 2. That I will say a good American "yes" and "no" in place of an
>   Indian grunt "um-hum" and "nup-um" or a foreign "ya" or
>   "yeh" and "nope."
> 3. That I will do my best to improve American speech by avoiding
>   loud rough tones, by enunciating distinctly, and by speaking
>   pleasantly, clearly, and sincerely.
> 4. That I will learn to articulate correctly as many words as possi-
>   ble during the year. (McDavid 1965, 9–10)

People familiar with the subsequent role of the NCTE in public
language debates may be surprised to hear of the organization's entry
on the side of prescriptivism, even overt nativism. But after this inaus-
picious launching, the NCTE promptly abjured popular, seat-of-the-

pants notions about American speech and committed itself to the scholarly study of language. By the late 1920s, the NCTE had already begun to sponsor and fund a historic series of scholarly studies of English usage which have formed our basic understanding of language in America (Leonard 1937; Marckwardt and Walcott 1938).

Although barely invented as a discipline at the time of the NCTE's founding, the new social science of linguistics provided by the middle of the century a solid empirical and theoretical base for public policy and educational practice in literacy instruction. Findings of linguists such as Leonard, Marckwardt, Bloomfield, Chomsky, and others offered rich insight into the nature of language, the origin and meaning of language differences, the process of language change, the centrality of linguistic identity to personal and cultural identity, and the kinds of school policies likely to help children develop optimally as readers and writers. Drawing upon this scholarly work, the NCTE has consistently worked to promote language policies in school and society that are appropriate, effective, respectful, pluralistic, and progressive.

While most of the NCTE's leadership in language and usage matters has been indirect, serving its teacher-members through research studies, curricula, and teaching materials, the Council's role has occasionally become more public. In 1974, toward the end of a long period of social change and civil rights struggle (as well as some key sociolinguistic research), the NCTE's Conference on College Communication and Composition passed a resolution called "Students' Right to Their Own Language" (Butler et al. 1974).

The SRTOL statement created a controversy that thrust NCTE into a bright and unfamiliar public spotlight. Many pundits and commentators outside the profession were enraged by the Council's allegedly radical stance. Language arbiter and columnist John Simon wrote: "One difficulty with addressing oneself to the absurdity of this pamphlet is that where every sentence . . . pullulates with logical and moral errors, one doesn't know where to begin with a rebuttal," and then he carried on for several hundred words about the irresponsibility of the NCTE (Simon 1980, 170–71).

But the point of the statement was simple, and looking back with sixteen years of retrospect, the document seems tamely factual and educationally unexceptionable. The SRTOL statement said that all human languages are of transcendent value to their speakers and that attacking the home language of schoolchildren is an alienating and unwise policy. Instead, the statement argued, teachers should respect, accept, and build upon whatever home language or dialect students bring with them to school. Nowhere did the statement reject the teaching of standard English; on the contrary, it assumed that students would want to learn the language of wider communication and that wise teachers would tap this motivation in the appropriate and timely teaching of the standard language.

National Language Policy in the 1990s

Today, in the controversy over the officialization of English, we are refighting the same old sociolinguistic issues—the struggles of the 1970s, the 1920s, and other times and places. If anything is certain about the current episode, it is this: in fifty years, when we look back upon all this turmoil, we will recognize the English-only furor of the 1980s and 1990s as another incident in the long history of American intolerance of immigrants and minorities, another outburst of our fear and hatred of the stranger. Our era will seem and sound much like the early 1920s, and we will immediately notice the remarkable structural similarities between the immigration patterns—the sudden and large influx of ethnically diverse people from unfamiliar areas of the world.

In 1919, it seemed inconceivable that the American nation could possibly assimilate millions of dark-skinned, poor, largely Catholic southern European immigrants without being "polluted" and destroyed. And yet, of course, we did gradually absorb all those peoples, and we have been immeasurably enriched in every aspect of our culture by doing so. Now those once-sinister Italians, Poles, and Jews have joined the old-timers in wondering: Can America absorb millions of Hispanics and Asians without being distorted, watered-down, and ruined?

Also when we look back fifty or seventy-five years from now, we will see that the English-only movement was built on misinformation, ignorance, and fear, but not on hatred. Whatever the politics of its leaders, the rank and file supporters, the ordinary citizens who marked official-English ballots and wrote small donation checks to U.S. English were not bigots. These were well-meaning, patriotic American citizens who supported language restrictionism out of genuine fear for the future of their country, or because they did not understand how language is actually learned and used, or because they had simply forgotten about the linguistic discrimination faced by their own immigrant ancestors. We will look back on the English-only movement, in other words, as a socially acceptable form of ethnic discrimination that passed from the scene just as soon as people understood its hidden meanings, its consequences, and the inhospitable messages it has sent to millions of our fellow citizens.

Works Cited

Bikales, Gerda. [Executive Director of U.S. English.] 1985. "Petition for FCC Rule Making." Letter. 26 September.

Butler, Melvin A., chair, and the Committee on the CCCC Language Statement. 1974. "Students' Right to Their Own Language." Special issue of *College Composition and Communication* 25 (Fall): 1–320.

Crawford, James. 1989. *Bilingual Education: History, Politics, Theory, and Practice.* Trenton, N.J.: Crane Publishing Company.

Davenport, Charles Benedict. 1911. *Heredity in Relation to Eugenics.* New York: Henry Holt and Company.

"English Only Law Becomes a Matter of Interpretation." 1989. *Chicago Tribune,* 15 January, 6.

EPIC Events (Newsletter of the English Plus Information Clearinghouse.) 1988. Washington, D.C.: January/February, March/April.

"Florida English." 1986. *Education Week,* 19 March.

"Frequently Used Arguments Against the Legal Protection of English." n.d. Flyer. Washington, D.C.: U.S. English.

Gavin, Jennifer. 1988. "Pena Outlaws Bias Based on Language," *Rocky Mountain News,* 29 December.

Hakuta, Kenji. 1986. *The Mirror of Language: The Debate on Bilingualism.* New York: Basic Books.

Horn, Jim. n.d. "English First" solicitation letter. Falls Church, Va.: Committee to Protect the Family.

Leonard, Sterling. 1937. *Current English Usage.* National Council of Teachers of English Monograph No. 1. Chicago: Inland.

Marckwardt, Albert H., and Fred G. Walcott. 1938. *Facts about Current Usage.* National Council of Teachers of English Monograph No. 7. New York: Appleton-Century.

McDavid, Raven, ed. 1965. *An Examination of the Attitudes of the NCTE Toward Language.* Champaign, Ill.: National Council of Teachers of English.

Robbins, Terry. 1985. "An Open Letter to All the Governors in the United States." Florida English Campaign, Dade County. 30 March.

Simon, John. 1980. *Paradigms Lost.* New York: Clarkson N. Potter.

Veltman, Clavin J. 1988. *The Future of the Spanish Language in the United States.* Washington, D.C.: Hispanic Policy Development Project.

Zall, Barnaby. n.d. "EL-PAC" solicitation letter.

2 The Legal Status of English in Illinois: Case Study of a Multilingual State

Dennis Baron
University of Illinois at Urbana-Champaign

The State of Illinois, more conservative than some states on language issues yet more liberal than others, furnishes an interesting case study for official-English and minority language legislation. Examining the discussion surrounding the language issues which Illinois has dealt with in the past, we find the same arguments and counterarguments surfacing once again. Two notions, one philosophical, the other nativist, sometimes joined, sometimes independent of one another, support official English in Illinois, as they have done in the United States for over two centuries: a perceived connection between American English and democratic social and political institutions, and more or less open hostility on the part of established Americans of European descent toward newer immigrant groups or other non-anglophone populations. Both notions assume English to be not simply a practical necessity for survival in an anglophone society, but the one essential badge of Americanism. While our laws and courts also tend to support official English, on the federal level and sometimes on the state level as well, they generally oppose efforts to discriminate on the basis of native language.

The result is the situation which pertains at the moment in Illinois, as it does in many other states, where English is declared to be the official language, while official efforts are made both to protect minority language speakers—though not necessarily the languages they speak—from discrimination and to assimilate them into the monolingual, anglophone mainstream. In addition, the state of Illinois supports the study of foreign languages in the schools, recognizing them, if not as essential to a universal liberal education, at least as an economic asset necessary for Illinois to compete in the worldwide economy.

Illinois has had an official-English law since 1923, though since its introduction the law has functioned exclusively in a symbolic capacity. And while Illinois declared English as the language of instruction in its schools more than a century ago, the state has consistently resisted efforts to curtail foreign language instruction. Although the legal history of language in Illinois may not reliably predict the outcome of federal official language legislation, it does show that the official language question has always been a volatile one, consistently evoking the issue of patriotism while masking racial, ethical, and religious intolerance.

English and the Illinois Constitution

Like most states in the Union, Illinois has dealt with the question of official English and the status of minority languages in its various state constitutions, where English is established as the language of government; in the school laws designating English as the language of instruction but explicitly permitting the study of foreign languages, and most recently, bilingual education as well; and in separate legislation designating the state's official language. While Illinois clearly puts English first, it makes room for minority languages as well. During the three periods in our nation's history when English-only movements pressured our legal and educational systems—the early 1890s, the period during and after World War I, and the present—Illinois has placed itself firmly in the middle of the road. The state has chosen English as its official language and its laws encourage transition to English rather than mother-tongue maintenance for minority language speakers. But official English in Illinois is symbolic rather than restrictive, and both official and informal support services, as well as native-language instruction, are available for nonanglophones.

The problem of language is addressed implicitly and explicitly throughout the legal history of the state. The fact that the Northwest Ordinance (1787) as well as the constitutions and laws of Illinois are written in English gives that language at least semiofficial status from the outset. However, from the outset, minority language groups asserted their rights as well: the French of Kaskaskia and Cahokia maintained separate courts in the 1780s. In 1794 the territorial laws were ordered translated into French so that the francophone judges could enforce them, and a French school was set up for one month in Cahokia. Shortly thereafter, the Cahokia French protested to Congress the abridgment both of their property rights (in particular, their right to keep slaves—slavery was prohibited by the Northwest Ordinance) and of their language rights ("Inquiry," 1796, 151; Allinson 1907, 281).

The first Illinois Constitution (1818) does not mention language, though Article II, Section 17 reads, "The style of the laws of this state shall be, 'Be it enacted by the people of the state of Illinois represented in the General Assembly,' "a phrase which makes clear that the state's laws will be drafted in English. More to the point, Schedule 18 of the Constitution of 1848 requires that "all laws of the State of Illinois, and all official writings, and the Executive, Legislative and Judicial proceedings, shall be conducted, preserved and published in no other than the English language" (Illinois 1847, 571). However, while the English-only requirement of Schedule 18 requires the formal record of all court proceedings to be in intelligible English, it does not restrict the language of such court proceedings as "oral testimony, depositions, or documentary evidence" (Illinois 1920, 305).

Both Schedule 18 and similar requirements set by other states have been construed by the courts to establish English as the presumptive official language of the states. In *Graham v. King* (1872), the Missouri Supreme Court interpreted a law requiring publication of foreclosure notices to mean printing of such notices *in English* in an *English-language* newspaper. This decision served as a precedent for later cases in Michigan and Illinois. The Missouri court assumed Americans to be monolingual: "An English advertisement in a German newspaper is bad. . . . Those among whom the [German] paper circulates would not be able to read it in the English language. And if it were published in German, then it would be a sealed book to the most of those who read and speak English." The Michigan Supreme Court went a step further, declaring, "the English language is the recognized language of this country, and whenever the law refers to publication in newspapers it means those published in the language of the country" (*Attorney General v. Hutchinson*, 1897).

In 1891 the Illinois Supreme Court invalidated earlier Chicago laws explicitly permitting or requiring official publication of notices in languages other than English (*McCoy v. City of Chicago*). Later the court struck down Chicago laws requiring publication of all official notices in English in the foreign language press. In *Perkins v. Commissioners* (1916), the complainant saw the existence of German newspapers as proof of German unwillingness to assimilate: "[They] adhere to the German language *in preference to* the language of this country" (emphasis added). The court agreed, citing the constitutional requirement of Schedule 18: "A notice or ordinance published in the English language in a newspaper printed in a foreign language cannot be said to be 'published,' in the sense in which that word is used in the constitution and laws of this State." In the related *People v. Day* (1917), the Illinois Supreme Court ruled that Day was not liable for that portion of his tax rendered void by publication of the tax levy in a German-language newspaper. Chicago city ordinances eventually came into line with such legal decisions, and with the anti-German feeling that swept the country during and after World War I. Since 1922, the city's Municipal Code has specified publication of required notices in an *English* newspaper, provided that newspaper does not advocate the overthrow of the government by force or violence.

While Illinois has privileged the English language through its laws, it has also been tolerant of the state's minority languages, even during periods in our history when other states were taking a more repressive view of the language question. Although during the nineteenth century the U.S. Congress rejected several attempts to have copies of the federal laws published in German or other languages, a proposal to publish 5,000 copies of the 1848 Illinois Constitution in German was overwhelmingly adopted, though a similar proposal to print copies "in the Irish and French languages" was soundly defeated. Delegates to the 1870 Constitutional Convention wanted their product to appear in the foreign-language press to ensure its adoption by the voters. Consequently the 1870 Illinois Constitution was ordered translated and printed in German, French, and "Scandinavian" (the exact meaning of the last term was left vague since the delegate proposing it claimed, "I am not particular about the languages. I do not read any of them"). However, a move to issue the document in Italian as well was rejected amid sarcastic cries of "Why not Chinese?" and "Why not African?" (Illinois 1870, 2: 1706; 1843–48).

The Language of Illinois Schools

Shortly before the first constitutional establishment of English in 1848, the 1845 School Law designated English as the language of instruction in Illinois schools. The official status of English was reaffirmed in later revisions of the school laws, which spelled out the right of schools to permit the teaching of other modern languages as well. According to the statute of 1845, "No school shall derive any benefit from the public or town fund unless the text books in said schools shall be in the English language, nor unless the common medium of communication in said schools shall be in the English language." Unlike most states, however, which banned foreign languages below the ninth grade, Illinois exempted foreign languages studied as such at any level from its English-only requirement. A law passed in 1869 further clarified the right of instructors to use a modern language as the vehicle for instruction in that modern language, a pedagogical technique whose importance seems self-evident today but which was clearly something in need of legal shoring-up a century ago.

The right to teach foreign languages in state public schools was successfully defended in *Powell v. Board of Education* (1881). In that case, a group of concerned citizens of St. Clair County sued the public school district to enjoin the use of public funds for German language instruction. The school in question offered a maximum of one hour per day of voluntary German, for which 80–90 percent of the pupils volunteered. Such instruction had been provided for some fifteen years, and the question had recently been approved at the polls as well. The Illinois Supreme Court concluded in its opinion that the teaching of modern languages in the state's public schools was legal, and that it did not diminish their character as English schools. Furthermore, the Court ruled that since the teaching of modern languages had been common in the elementary branches for many years, it would take legislative rather than judicial action to forbid such instruction.

The Edwards Law

Perhaps in response to this finding, in 1889 the Illinois legislature passed with little fanfare or opposition a law requiring English as the language of instruction in all public and parochial schools. Known as the Edwards Law, after the State Superintendent of Public Instruction, it split the state along philosophical, ethnic, religious, and party lines. Opponents of the law were attacked as enemies of public education and were the objects of violent anti-Catholic, anti-Democrat, and anti-German attacks in the press. In language that paves the way for supporters of today's official language statutes, the *Chicago Tribune* praised Republican supporters of the Edwards Law for refusing to believe "that an elementary education is sufficient with the American tongue left out, or forbidden to be taught to the American children of narrow-minded, un-American foreigners." The *Tribune* warned that the Democrats would even go so far as to support the complete exclusion of English from the schools if they thought it would get them votes (June 14, 1891, 12).

Opposition to the Edwards Law produced a political alliance of two groups concerned with maintaining control over their own parochial schools: German Lutherans, who normally voted Republican, and Catholics. This coalition managed to defeat Edwards in his bid for re-election as school superintendent, replacing him with a Democrat who happened also to be a German American. In 1892 John P. Altgeld made the school language issue a central feature of his gubernatorial campaign, and the Democrats managed to end twenty years of Republican rule in the state. The Edwards Law was repealed in 1893, and a new compulsory attendance law was implemented without the English language provision—at least for the time being (Kučera 1955).

The Effects of World War I

American attitudes toward minority languages have a history of swinging between extremes of tolerance and intolerance. During and after World War I, negative feeling toward German, Polish, Czech, and the Scandinavian languages resurfaced, particularly in the Midwest. America entered the war in April, 1917. Over the next few months, a language panic swept the country. Reacting to charges that the German government was underwriting language instruction in American schools to prevent the assimilation of German-Americans and further its war effort, and that German classes were hotbeds of subversion and espionage, school districts throughout the nation promptly banned the teaching of German. As many as twenty-five states had removed German from their curricula by June of 1918.

Perhaps most drastic of all, and most indicative of public sentiment at the time, was the proclamation of Iowa Governor W. S. Harding, issued in May, 1918, forbidding the use of any foreign language in the schools, in public, or on the telephone, a more public instrument then than it is now. Harding even went so far as to prescribe English as the official language of religion:

> English should and must be the only medium of instruction in public, private, denominational and other similar schools. Conversation in public places, on trains, and over the telephone should be in the English language. Let those who cannot speak or understand the English language conduct their religious worship in their home. (*New York Times*, June 18, 1918, p. 12)

According to James Crawford (1989, 23), as many as 18,000 people were charged in the Midwest with violating English-only statutes.

The Illinois Constitutional Convention of 1920–22

While legislation in Illinois affirmed the position of English as the one official language of government and education, the state resisted the temptation to restrict minority language rights: German did not flourish in Illinois schools or on its streets between 1917 and 1920, but neither was it banned.

The Illinois Constitutional Convention of 1920–22 dealt with the language issue in three major areas: literacy, the courts, and the schools. The delegates wrote into the new constitution an English literacy requirement for all appointed and elected officeholders, while rejecting a broader literacy test for voting. They affirmed English as the official language of the laws and public records of the state. And they rejected requiring English as the language of instruction in the schools. Their consideration of the language issue mirrors similar discussions in New York State and Pennsylvania at the time, and it will sound familiar to those following today's debates over official-English legislation.

The Question of English Literacy

The Constitutional Convention overwhelmingly endorsed a requirement that public officeholders, whether appointed or elected, be able to speak, read, and write English. Sylvester J. Gee, the Republican delegate who spearheaded the literacy drive, felt it was the patriotic duty of such officeholders to speak English. One opponent objected that English was not necessary for public jobs like road supervisor and expressed concern about the accurate measurement of literacy. Others feared the requirement might work as a racial and ethnic barrier, but it was passed nonetheless.

Gee and his supporters sought to make English literacy a requirement for voting as well, but this proved much more controversial. Opponents argued that a literacy requirement would disenfranchise many blacks and non-English-speaking patriots who had fought in the Civil War and the recently concluded Great War. A Chicago delegate protested that many of his black constituents had not been well served by the schools, and he feared they would reject a constitution with a literacy clause. But the paternalistic Gee denied that blacks had been mistreated: "In my county they sit in the same schools. I have a young man in my employment who is a bright colored boy. He has had the same opportunity as any white child, and he is able to read and write." As for the foreign born, Gee argued, "I do not ask anything of them that is not asked of American-born citizens, and I do not think it is asking too much that they be able to read and write the language of their country" (Illinois 1920–22, 997).

Another Chicago delegate, who was himself an immigrant, saw the English literacy requirement for voting as "an affront to the people who have not had an adequate opportunity to learn to write and read the English language, but who are nevertheless willing and desirous of

becoming loyal citizens" (997–98). And a Bloomington delegate eloquently objected to the unfair treatment of veterans under a literacy
requirement: "To disfranchise certain men who in the darkest hour
that this nation ever saw went out with their lives in their hands ready
to do and die for our flag, would be an infernal disgrace" (998). This was
apparently enough for Gee, who allowed the question of literacy to be
dropped from the voting rights section of the constitution.

The Language of the Schools

Sparking a debate that in many ways parallels today's bilingual education controversy, Lewis A. Jarman, a Republican delegate from Rush-
ville, put forward a motion to require English as the language of instruction in all public and private schools. Jarman argued that English-
first laws were necessary to protect the nation "from the insidious
wiles of foreign influence," a phrase recalling George Washington's
warning against international entanglements. Jarman remarked that
Washington never imagined the need to protect the English language
from " 'the insidious wiles' of modern Germany" (Illinois 1920–22,
1140). Although he would permit German in the school curriculum
and did not oppose foreign language instruction as such, Jarman did
single out German as a problem for American schools:

> We have needed the alarm of war to awaken us to the significance
> of the fact that in some cities and communities of this country we
> have elementary schools where German is the only language
> spoken, except in that room where English is taught as a foreign
> language. . . . I think it is a reproach to any community of the
> United States, and a reflection upon its loyalty to American ideas,
> to have, not simply a public elementary school where German is
> taught, but to have German public elementary schools. (1140–41)

Jarman then set forth the oft-repeated one-nation, one-language
doctrine. For him, language replaced ethnicity as the primary unit of
social and political cohesion: "In this country national unity is not a
matter of blood but of ideas. . . . American ideas have been born in
English and require English for their proper preservation and dissemination" (1140). And since in his opinion the goal of public education
was national unity itself, any tolerance of minority languages threatened the national fabric: "How shall we ever make these millions think
American if we do not teach them to speak American?" Ironically, the
nation-language connection so effectively disseminated through German romantic language philosophy backfired as Jarman touted English as the language of democracy while characterizing German as an
antidemocratic, warlike tongue, which threatened American national

unity: "If we permit the children and citizens to live, move and have their intellectual being in the language and literature of absolutism (i.e., German), it will be well nigh hopeless to attempt to preserve a pure democracy among them" (1141).

In another warning that presages today's language debates, Jarman concluded his passionate, prepared speech by raising the specter of Babel and "the disintegrating tendencies of polyglot States" (1141). While he claimed to oppose an "America for Americans" immigration policy, he rejected any notion of minority language maintenance and drew applause from the convention with a final equation of English with liberty:

> He is a public enemy who would in any way hinder (the schools) from teaching American ideas, cherishing American ideals, promoting American patriotism, and above all, producing American citizens, unhyphenated and uncompromising, a united democracy loving liberty, and thinking and speaking the language of liberty, our English undefiled. (1142)

The emotion stirred by Jarman's prepared remarks was quickly deflated when delegate Frank S. Whitman of Belvidere reminded the convention that the previous legislature had already reinstated English as the language of school instruction (see below), and Jarman's amendment failed to pass. But it was clear to all that the sentiment of the delegates favored protecting English when such a move did not threaten to alienate non-English speaking voters. There was little discussion, for example, about renewing Schedule 18 (Illinois 1920-22, 4523). Breaking with tradition, moreover, the 1920-22 Constitutional Convention did not authorize the publication of the new constitution in any language other than English, and in 1923 Illinois passed its first official-language law.

Ryan's Law

Postwar official-English sentiment was colored to some extent by the anti-British feeling of many Irish-Americans. In 1923, Montana Representative Washington Jay McCormick introduced a bill in the U.S. Congress to make *American* the nation's official tongue. McCormick's foe was not so much the Kaiser as the King. Hoping to "supplement the political emancipation of '76 by the mental emancipation of '23," he advised our writers to "drop their top-coats, spats, and swagger-sticks, and assume occasionally their buckskin, moccasins, and tomahawks" (Baron 1982, 40).

McCormick's bill died in committee, but American was clearly in the air in 1923. State Senator Frank Ryan of Chicago sponsored a law making American—not English—the official language of Illinois. Opposition to all things English was spearheaded by Chicago Mayor William Hale ("Big Bill") Thompson, and its result is clear in the wording of Ryan's official language law, whose *whereases*—which were toned down in the final version of the bill—attack those American Tories "who have never become reconciled to our republican institutions and have ever clung to the tradition of King and Empire," defeating the attempts of American patriots "to weld the racial units into a solid American nation."

Despite its passage, and whatever its sponsor's intent, the Illinois official language law produced no sweeping changes in usage in the state, where English rather than American continued to be taught in the public schools, albeit illegally. In 1928, the Illinois Appeals Court regularized the terminology conflict, ruling that the official *American* law did not conflict with the constitutional requirement that Illinois laws be published in English because the languages were "in legal effect and intendment . . . the same thing" (Leideck v. City of Chicago). One effect of Ryan's law, though, was to make Illinois language terminology unique among the states, and the statute was quietly amended in 1969 to restore English as the official state language (Illinois Public Act 76-1464).

The Illinois School Code

Twenty years after the Edwards Law controversy, at the urging of Samuel Insull, chair of the wartime State Council of Defense of Illinois, the Illinois legislature in 1919 revised the school code and English once again became the official language of instruction in the state's public and parochial schools. Section 276a of the new school code embodied the language of Insull's Defense Council:

> Because the English language is the common as well as official language of our country, and because it is essential to good citizenship that each citizen shall have or speedily acquire, as his natural tongue, the language in which the laws of the land, the decree of the courts, and the proclamations and pronouncements of its officials are made, and shall easily and naturally think in the language in which the obligations of his citizenship are defined, the instruction in the elementary branches of education in all schools in Illinois shall be in the English language. (Insull 1919a)

Like many of his contemporaries, Insull considered English-language schools the most important component of the Americanization process. In a speech on the subject, he warned that ever since Babel, multilingualism had been a subversive activity: "A confusion of tongues is the simplest and most effective method for defeating a common purpose yet discovered; it was the method employed by Jehovah himself to accomplish that end" (Insull 1919b, 465). Insull would permit first-generation immigrants their native tongues, and he did not object to the teaching of foreign languages in the schools of Illinois, though he strongly objected to foreign language schools and the minority language maintenance they attempted to provide: "There is no reason why we should go on maintaining and propagating the babel of languages through the second, and even the third and fourth, generations." According to Insull, if we fail to provide an elementary curriculum in English, "we deliberately make [immigrant children] poor Americans by allowing them to acquire their education in a foreign tongue" (465). He concluded, "We can't make a foreign-born citizen a good American by law. But we can make the schools of Illinois American by law, and thereby make it easier for those born here to be good Americans" (466).

In 1920, the same year that the Modern Language Association, meeting in Columbus, Ohio, urged Congress to support foreign language instruction, Illinois tried to extend its English-only school law to the rest of the nation. Representative Charles E. Fuller, of the Illinois 12th Congressional District, transmitted a petition from the Illinois Society of the Sons of the American Revolution to the U.S. House of Representatives "favoring the teaching only of the English language in elementary schools" (*Congressional Record,* 1920). The House Committee on Education did not act on the measure.

Conclusion

Despite the well-publicized Americanization policy of the United States during and after World War I, the nation's schools were not well prepared to de-hyphenate immigrant children, or even to teach them English, although many children managed to learn the language anyway. Citing statistics from Chicago and other regions, Colin Greer (1972) shows that more immigrant children failed in school than succeeded, and large numbers of them dropped out altogether. American educational authorities did not develop specialized English teaching materials for non-anglophone children, nor did they prepare teachers much beyond giving them short lists of the types of pronunciation or idiom errors that supposedly characterized the different ethnic groups. Adult education fared no better: what few facilities there were existed only in urban areas, and the sole qualifications a teacher needed to teach in them were the ability to speak English and the desire for overtime pay.

Today's language minorities fared little better than their predecessors until the Bilingual Education Act of 1968 and the Lau decision of 1974 forced authorities to address the specific educational needs of limited-English proficiency children. Illinois adopted a bilingual education law in 1973. The most recent amendment of the Illinois School Code was made to bring that section of state law into line with already-existing state and federally mandated bilingual education programs. The statute now reads, "Instruction in all public elementary and secondary schools of the State shall be in the English language except in second language programs and except in conjunction with programs which the school board may provide, with the approval of the State Board of Education pursuant to Article 14C, in a language other than English for children whose first language is other than English" (1988 Illinois Public Act 85-1389).

Bilingual education is now legal in Illinois, and while it is almost certain to be transitional in nature, the School Code does not rule out minority-language maintenance programs. But the future of bilingual education is uncertain. Supporters of English-only legislation such as the English Language Amendment to the U.S. Constitution (the ELA) oppose bilingual programs, fearing the proliferation not of German but of Spanish. By linking immigration with the question of a national language, the current English-first debate does not differ much from earlier attempts to deal with the fact that the United States is and has always been a multilingual country whose basic language is English.

As the balance of Illinois legal history shows, an official language designation may be purely symbolic. However, today's bilingual education programs exist because English-only school laws often served as excuses for the schools to permit non-English-speaking students to sink rather than swim. The ELA and similar state laws could add to the already negative climate for bilingualism and minority language maintenance, impede transition to English, and discourage much-needed foreign language instruction in this country.

The fact that Illinois language law is currently functioning both permissively and symbolically may not prevent it from taking an English-only direction in the future. An extreme interpretation of the ELA, for example, might not only outlaw foreign language requirements in college curricula, it could also prevent the voluntary teaching of any foreign language except for the limited purpose of helping a non-English speaker to learn English (Dale 1985). It should be noted, however, that Arizona, whose recent official language law is one of the nation's most restrictive, requiring that "this state and all political subdivisions of this state shall act in English and no other language," specifically permits both transitional bilingual education and school foreign language requirements. Furthermore, shortly after the passage of the new Arizona law, that state's Attorney General issued an opinion that "it does not prohibit the use of languages other than English that are reasonably necessary to facilitate the day-to-day operation of government" (Crawford 1989, 67–68).

Ironically, official-English laws are not needed as tools to suppress minority languages, for as Fishman et al. (1985) have shown, even in the absence of restrictive legislation, minority languages in the United States have always been marginal, if not completely doomed. Rather, the true danger of official language legislation is that such laws may not only fail to facilitate the adoption of English, they may actually deter the learning of English by isolating non-English speakers further from the American mainstream. The framers of the federal Constitution, who dealt with the same problems of multilingualism that face us today, chose to adopt an informal English-first policy rather than an English-only law (see Baron, forthcoming). Their attitude should lead us to question the necessity of official language legislation whose purpose seems not linguistic but culturally and politically isolationist in its thrust.

Works Cited

Cases Cited

Attorney General v. Hutchinson. 1897. 113 Mich. 245.
Graham v. King. 1872. 50 Mo. 22.
Lau v. Nichols. 1974. 414 U.S. Reports 563.
Leideck v. City of Chicago. 1928. 248 Ill. App. 545.
McCoy v. City of Chicago. 1891. 136 Ill. 344.
Meyer v. Nebraska. 1923. 262 U.S. 390.
Perkins v. Board of Commissioners of Cook County. 1916. 271 Ill. 449.
People v. Day. 1917. 277 Ill. 543.
Powell v. Board of Education. 1881. 97 Ill. 375.

Other Works Cited

Allinson, May. 1907. "The Government of Illinois, 1790–1799." *Transactions of the Illinois State Historical Society* 12: 277–92.

Baron, Dennis. Forthcoming. *The English-Only Question: An Official Language for Americans?*

———. 1982. *Grammar and Good Taste: Reforming the American Language.* New Haven: Yale University Press.

Chicago Tribune. 1891. 14 June, 12.

Congressional Record. 1920. 66th Congress, 1st Session, 23 March.

Crawford, James. 1989. *Bilingual Education: History, Politics, Theory, and Practice.* Trenton, N.J.: Crane Publishing.

Dale, Charles V. 1985. "Legal Analysis of S. J. Res. 167 and H. J. Res. 169 Proposing an Amendment to the U.S. Constitution to Make English the Official Language of the United States. In *The English Language Amendment: Hearing before the Subcommittee on the Constitution of the Committee on the Judiciary, U.S. Senate,* 32–35; 89–95. Washington, D.C.: Government Printing Office.

Fishman, Joshua, et. al. 1985. *The Rise and Fall of the Ethnic Revival: Perspectives on Language and Ethnicity.* Berlin: Mouton.

Greer, Colin. 1972. *The Great School Legend: A Revisionist Interpretation of American Public School Education.* New York: Basic Books.

State of Illinois. 1920. *Constitution of the State of Illinois, Annotated.* Springfield: Legislative Reference Bureau.

———. 1870. *Debates and Proceedings of the Constitutional Convention of the State of Illinois.* Springfield.

———. 1847. *Journal of the Convention Assembled at Springfield, June 7, 1847.* Springfield.

———. 1920–22. *Proceedings of the Constitutional Convention of the State of Illinois.* 5 vols. Springfield: Illinois State Journal Company.

"Inquiry into the Official Conduct of a Judge of the Supreme Court of the Northwest Territory." 1796. *American State Papers,* 1834. Ser. 10, vol. 1, no. 89: 151–52. Washington, D.C.: 1834.

Insull, Samuel. 1919a. *Final Report of the State Council of Defense of Illinois 1917–1918-1919.* N.p.: State of Illinois.

———. 1919b. Speech to the Commercial Club of Chicago (18 January). *Illinois in the World War,* edited by Marguerite E. Jenison, vol. 6, 456–66. Springfield: Illinois State Historical Society, 1923.

Kučera, Daniel W. 1955. "Church-State Relationships in Education in Illinois." *Catholic University of America Educational Research Monographs* 19: 1. Washington, D.C.: Catholic University of America Press.

New York Times. 1918. 18 June, 12.

3 Metaphors and Motives of Language-Restriction Movements

Elizabeth Frick
Applied Learning Systems

Water images appear recurrently in contemporary reports of immigration and English-only issues.[1] The immigration of non-English speakers is almost always described as a problem, but with remarkable consistency it is seen more specifically as a *disaster by water:* a flood, a tide, a flow, a wave, a stream, a deluge, an inundation that threatens to drown the country. For example, a recent news story in *The Houston Post* claimed that

> a new immigration reform law was signed last week providing amnesty for many people who arrived illegally in the past, but imposing employer sanctions and other provision in the hope of stemming future *flow* of illegal arrivals. (Balk 1986, 10C)[2]

A *Newsweek* subheading warned:

> America has "lost control" of its borders, but remains deeply divided over how to curb the inexorable *flood* of illegal immigration—and still be true to the open-door tradition that helped to build the country. (Morganthau 1984, 18)

In the same article, a captioned question reads "Would the *flood* of illegals taint their welcome?" (19). In addition, a graph delineating periods of immigration since 1830 is entitled, "A Rising *Tide* Again," and subtitled, "When the estimated *flood* of illegal immigrants is included, the number of foreigners now settling in the United States is approaching its historical peak" (22). Irish immigration on the graph is referred to as "The *influx* from Ireland"; Chinese immigration in 1880 is called "A *tide* from China [which] outlasted the railroad-building era."

Similarly, a headline in a university paper warns: "Foreign Grad Students *Flood* U.S. Colleges" ("Foreign Grad Students," 1987, 1). In 1983, *Time* magazine warned: "The statistical evidence of the immigrant *tide* is stark" (Andersen 1983, 19). A book about immigration insists that "there is a *flood* of people rising right outside our door" (Lamm and Imhoff 1985, 8).

Even *The New Republic* employs unflattering aquatic metaphors in an editorial about immigration: "Once preoccupied with borders so *porus* that everything from drugs to communism could *seep* across ..." ("Immigration Reform II," 1987, 7).

Water images in English-only articles always seem to threaten potential disaster, and immigrants are always dangerous:

> Can Miami cope with new *flood* of refugees? (Chaze 1989, 55)

> The United States is receiving the largest *wave* of immigration in its history. (Wright 1983b, B9)

> Language *logjam*: students *swamp* English classes. (Garcia 1986, 1)

> If the new *wave* of immigrants is unable to meet the standards and the challenges this country offers ... the answer is to remind them that fishing boats can sail both ways, and that a river can be crossed in both directions. (Ben Hall 1984, S728)

> The Supreme Court ruled in a key 1974 decision (*Lau vs. Nicholes* [sic] that opened the bilingual *floodgates*. (*English First Solicitation Letter*, 1986)

> By joining our organization you will become part of an active network of concerned citizens determined to stop the mindless *drift* toward a bilingual America. (Bikales, "Dear Friend," n.d.)

> In heavily Hispanic South Florida, the issue has become so inflamed that it now *spills over* into unrelated matters. (Alter 1984, 24)

> All this indicates that Americans are deeply concerned about the *erosion* of English they see all around us. (Symms 1985, S515)

> This *influx* strains our facilities for assimilation. (Wright 1983b, B9)

> The feeling among some people is that, now that we're here, let's just pull up the *gangplank* and keep the others out. (Chaze 1989, 55)

> But America is poorly equipped with the rising *tide* of people seeking to come to the United States. ("Immigration and the National Interest," 1987, 2)

It seems clear that immigrants are very regularly painted in a negative light through the use of disaster-by-water images in contemporary prose. Is this a new technique? Or, as Harry Truman (1955) suggested, should we look at the precedents? By looking back, Truman found

> that the history [of] the world has moved in cycles and that very often we find ourselves in the midst of political circumstances which appear to be new but which might have existed in almost identical form at various times during the past six thousand years

.... History taught me about the periodic wave of hysteria which started with the witch craze during colonial days, produced the abominable Alien and Sedition Acts of the 1790s, flourished again in the Know-Nothing movement, the anti-Masonic hysteria, anti-Catholicism, the Ku Klux Klan, the Red scare of 1919. When the cycle repeated itself during my administration in the form of anti-Communist hysteria and indiscriminate branding of innocent persons as subversives, I could deal with the situation calmly because I knew something of its background.... (120–21)

To determine if we are viewing a "cycle repeat[ing] itself," it helps to compare the metaphors employed today with those that appear in historical discussions about immigration. But first, a brief review of immigration history will provide a context for understanding the metaphors and motives of earlier periods.

For approximately the first hundred years of our national history, the United States was open to immigration from all countries without restriction. However, immigrants were not universally welcomed. For example, in 1793, Benjamin Franklin wrote about immigrants: "Unless the *stream* of their importation could be turned from this to other colonies...." In other discussions, foreigners were referred to as coming from "reservoirs":

Here was another Asiatic *reservoir* of over 300 million souls threatening to *deluge* the coast. (Stoddard 1921, 45)

There were three historic "peaks" in the immigration process: the Irish, Russian Jews, Germans, Swedes, Norwegians, Sicilians and Neapolitans, who immigrated from about 1830 to 1854; the Chinese immigration, which spanned from about 1880 to 1900; and the eastern and southern European immigration, which occurred in the first quarter of the twentieth century.

Eruptions of nativism (defined as hostility to immigrants) coincided with each main period of immigration. Know-nothingism flourished in the early 1850s, expressed in terms of the no-Popery tradition. The next surge of nativism was expressed not in Protestant terms but in economic and political terms during the late-nineteenth-century depression. Finally, nativism accelerated in the first two decades of the twentieth century, when influential eugenicists like Madison Grant and Lothrop Stoddard asserted that all other peoples were inferior to the Nordic race.

The first restrictive immigration laws appeared in 1882 and were directed against the Chinese on the West Coast. One example was a San Francisco ordinance which declared dwelling units illegal if rented with less than 500 cubic feet of air per person. The law was used to jail

Chinese residents in conditions which violated the order (Chan 1981, 15). A second period of restrictive legislation culminated in 1907 with the "gentlemen's agreement" to limit Asian immigration. A third period of legislative control resulted in a 1924 decision to freeze the ethnic and racial composition of the United States by restricting immigration to countries of northwestern Europe (British, Germans, and Irish) and limit southern and eastern Europeans to extremely scant quotas. Asians were banned entirely, and the quotas thwarted immigration by Jews from Europe (Brogan 1985).

Looking back over the writings of these times, we find water images repeatedly linked to immigration. Hugh Brogan (1985), author of *The Longman History of the United States of America* wrote: "The immigration came in three great *tides*, each stronger than the last. The first *rose* in the 1830s and 1840s to a *high-water* mark in 1854" (413–14). Others, too, used sea images in discussing immigration: "The report urges some action of legislature, if any is practicable, by which the *tide* of pauper and criminal immigration can be checked" (Busey 1856). Still other nativists employed images of streams and floods:

> Watch the gopher at work. He starts to bore into a levee, and as he progresses he is joined by more of his kind; then, in due time, the other side of the embankment is reached, and a little *stream* passes through. As the dirt crumbles, a *flow* increases and unless promptly checked, the bore soon becomes a wide gap with the *water* rushing through and *overflowing* the land. That is the *flood* that means loss, and perhaps eventual disaster. That is exactly what is happening in the State of California today through the Japanese policy of peaceful penetration. (Chambers 1921, 25)

Also from the same era:

> The *flood* came in [1900–14] too fast and it settled in congested areas. It appears to many very doubtful whether we could in any proper sense and in any reasonable length of time assimilate and Americanize a new *flood tide* from southern and eastern Europe. (National Committee, 1921, 212)

And in 1920, Lothrop Stoddard warned that the Aryan races were endangered by *The Rising Tide of Color*:

> The upshot is that the rising *flood* of color finds itself walled in by white *dikes* debarring it from many a promised land which it would fain *deluge* with its dusky *waves*. (83)

Other images used to refer to immigrants did not center on disaster by water but used other derogatory water images:

> When that great *reservoir* of cheap labor was opened [Chinese immigration] and when its *streams* began to *pour* into the United States the American people, first on the Western coast, and then elsewhere, suddenly were roused to the fact that they were threatened with a *flood* of low-class labor which would absolutely destroy good wages among American workingmen.... (Lodge 1891)

> Wherever the Japanese have settled, their nests *pollute* the communities like the running sores of leprosy. They exist like the yellowed, smoldering, discarded butts in an over-filled ashtray, vilifying the air with their loathsome smells, filling all who have misfortune to look upon them with a wholesome disgust and a desire to wash. ("The American Defender," 1935, 70)

Obviously, such overtly racist arguments would not be permissible in most mainstream publications, today. But even as far back as one hundred years ago, the idea of using language differences as a more polite pretext for fundamentally hateful sentiments was entertained as a possibility. Such sentiments were expressed in an editorial appearing in *The Nation* in 1891, entitled, "The Proper Sieve for Immigrants":

> We do not pretend to be wiser on this subject than anyone else, but if it be decided that unrestricted immigration, as at present carried on, is dangerous to American institutions and ideals, it is very odd that the value of language as a political and moral test of fitness should be more easily applied than any other.... This test would shut out more of the undesirable element in immigration. It is true, it would to a great extent confine immigration to English, Scotch, and Irishmen, but why not, if the restriction be really undertaken in the interest of American civilization? ("The Proper Sieve," 1891, 312)

Images in the prose of the 1980s mirror the water metaphors of old. For example, a contemporary writer likens an immigrant child to a fish in a stream:

> We had a youngster come from Haiti. The Board of Education wasn't about to hire a French teacher to teach him academics in French. They *mainstreamed* him. He *flip-flopped* and *floundered* for about a semester, but after that he forged right ahead with the rest of the kids. (English First Members' Report, 1986, 2)

Subsequently, the image is extended to all immigrant children:

> Now even the parents of some immigrant children are backing moves to *plunge* them into classes conducted in English-only, similar to the *immersion* process of past decades when *waves* of new-

comers flocked to America and rapidly joined the *mainstream*. (Solorzano 1984, 24)

According to English-only advocates, immigrants threaten to erode
the English language:

> All this indicates that Americans are deeply concerned about the
> *erosion* of English they see all around us. (Symms 1985, S515)

> Could America survive if the English language were to *erode*? (Ger-
> da Bikales 1983a)

It is not surprising that immigrants would be linked with sea images, for, on a simple and conscious level, most immigrants traveled
here by water. What is interesting is the synechdochic rhetorical jump
to the next level of consciousness: immigrants (who came by water)
threaten America with economic and psychological disaster. In a
country in which we all came from somewhere else, America is not the
mother country and English is not everyone's mother tongue. Immigrants are a reminder of that reality, and the leaders of the English-
only movement evoke images of anima and water, drawing on arche-
typal fears of returning to the "womb" of the mother country.[3]

If this is true, then it is no mistake that our lexicon links language
issues to water: we describe language ability as *fluency*, using a word
whose etymology (Latin: *fluo, fluere*) means "to flow." We urge that
non-native speakers move into the *mainstream* linguistically; and we
suggest that *immersion* is the pedagogy of choice. One's native language is one's "mother tongue."

Rejection of the mother tongue and culture seems to motivate many
individual leaders of the English-only movement who have been per-
secuted on racial/linguistic grounds. S. I. Hayakawa, whose parents
emigrated from Japan to Canada and then to the United States, was
denied full-time college teaching positions in the United States for
fifteen years because of anti-Japanese sentiment during the 1940s and
1950s. Later, Hayakawa's statements as a U.S. Senator revealed much
of his ideology. He claimed that the United States' internment of
116,000 Japanese-Americans in World War II was "perhaps the best
thing that could have happened" because it integrated the Japanese
into mainstream American society (Hume 1979, 4).

Like Hayakawa, Gerda Bikales, former executive director of U.S.
English, also experienced ethnic discrimination directly. Bikales, a Jew
whose native language was German, escaped Nazi Germany. "As a
young child in Nazi-occupied Europe," she wrote, "I had to learn
languages (Flemish and French) as a matter of survival" (Bikales 1983b,
22).

A third leader of the movement to declare English "official" was Emmy Shafer, who led the Miami petition drive in 1980 to abolish the use of Spanish in official documents. Ms. Shafer was born in the Soviet Union and spent time in a concentration camp during World War II before emigrating to the United States at the age of sixteen. In 1980 she was quoted as saying:

> I love Miami—the way it was at the time . . . unbelievable. Friendly, no problems. You didn't feel you were in a foreign country. [I want Miami back] the way it used to be [before the Mariel boatlift]. (Thomas 1980, 26)

It seems evident by now that this past decade's English-only movement is another cycle of nativism, another "wave" of anti-immigrant rhetoric, this time explicitly linked to language issues. Unfortunately, in this "United States of Amnesia," as Gore Vidal (1988) refers to us, the historical lesson is never quite as obvious as we would like it to be.

The fundamental lesson is this: when a climate of hatred is created, real people get discriminated against, deprived, devalued, and hurt. This understanding helps us make sense, among other things, of the horrific 1988 news story in which a drifter opened fire ("School Gunman," 1985, 1A) with an assault rifle on a crowded California school yard, killing five children of Southeast Asian refugees, because, as he later stated, he hated Asian immigrants and believed they were robbing native-born Americans of jobs.

Notes

1. I have found the following images linked to immigrants in both contemporary and historical press: bridge, bulwark, dikes, deluge, drifting, drown, dumping ground, erode/erosion, ebb and flow, flood, flow, gangplank, infusion, inundation, influx, low-water mark, leaks, mainstream, pouring/pour-in, peak, pollute, reservoirs, rudder, shipwrecked, "sink-or-swim," spawn, spill over, stagnation, stream, submerged, submersion, surge, swamped, swarming, swell, tide, wave.

Although I wish I could claim that exceptional research techniques were employed to locate these images, I must admit that I used merely ordinary methods: I saved copies of current articles in which these metaphors appeared, and I spent about six hours browsing through the journal shelves in the Wilson Library at the University of Minnesota where I found the historical quotes. I used no electronic retrieval or search techniques or interlibrary loans. I hope that this statement will be interpreted as indicative of how prevalent and easily uncovered are the examples of anti-immigrant water and disaster imagery.

2. All italics applied to water imagery have been supplied by the author.

3. I am grateful to Tess Galati, of Practical Communications, Inc., for the Jungian insights she contributed to this article.

Works Cited

Alter, Jonathan. 1984. "English Spoken Here, Please." *Newsweek*, 9 January.

"American Defender." 1944. In *Prejudice and Japanese Americans: Symbol of Racial Intolerance*, edited by Carey McWilliams, 68–70. Boston: Little, Brown.

Andersen, Kurt. "The New Ellis Island." 1983. *Time*, 13 June, 18–27.

Balk, Diane M. 1986. "Hot Line Fields Grammar Questions." *The Houston Post*, 13 November, 10C.

Bikales, Gerda. n.d. "Dear Friend." Solicitation letter from U.S. English. Washington, D.C.: U.S. English.

———. 1983a. "United States Moving Toward a Bilingual Society?" *English Around the World*, 29, no. 4.

———. 1983b. "You'd Be a Nobody If They Didn't Make You Learn English." *Christian Science Monitor*, 20 April, 22.

Brogan, Hugh. 1985. *The Longman History of the United States of America*. New York: Morrow.

Busey, Samuel C. 1856. *Immigration: Its Evils and Consequences*. New York: DeWitt & Davenport.

Chambers, John S. 1921. "The Japanese Invasion." In *Present-Day Immigration with Special Reference to the Japanese. The Annals of the American Academy of Political and Social Science*, vol. 93 (January), edited by Karl Kelsey, 211–24. Philadelphia: University of Pennsylvania.

Chan, Sucheng. 1981. "Public Policy, U.S.-China Relations, and the Chinese American Experience: An Interpretive Essay." In *Pluralism, Racism, and Public Policy: The Search for Equality*, edited by Edwin G. Clausen and Jack Bermingham, 5–38. Boston: G. K. Hall.

Chaze, William L. 1989. "Can Miami Cope with New Flood of Refugees?" *U.S. News and World Report*, 12 May, 55–56.

English First Solicitation Letter. 1986.

English First Members' Report. 1986. Vol. 1, no. 2 (December). Sacramento, Ca.

"Foreign Grad Students Flood U.S. Colleges." 1987. *Minnesota Daily*, 30 September, 1.

Franklin, Benjamin. 1840. [1793.] "Letter to Peter Collinson." In *The Works of Benjamin Franklin*, vol. 7, edited by Jared Sparks, 66–73. Boston: Hilliard, Gray, and Co.

Hall, Ben. 1984. "English as the Official Language." Madisonville (KY) *Messenger*, 25 January. Rpt. in *Congressional Record*, 98th Cong. 2d Sess. Vol. 130: S728.

Horn, Jim. "Letter" to Fellow Americans on English First Letterhead. n.d.

Hume, Ellen. 1979. "1000 Japanese-Americans Hit Hayakawa in Newspaper Ad." *Los Angeles Times*, 10 May, II, 4.

"Immigration and the National Interest." 1987. *Newsletter of the American Immigration Control Foundation,* July/August.

"Immigration Reform II." 1987. *New Republic.* 30 March, 7–8.

Lamm, Richard, and Gary Imhoff. 1985. *The Immigration Time Bomb: The Fragmenting of America.* New York: Truman Talley.

Lodge, Henry Cabot. 1891. "The Restriction of Immigration." *North American Review* 152: 27–36.

Morganthau, Tom. 1984. *Newsweek,* 25 June, 18+.

National Committee for Constructive Immigration Legislation. 1921. "New Flood Tide of Immigration: A Policy and a Program." In *Present-Day Immigration with Special Reference to the Japanese. The Annals of the American Academy of Political and Social Science,* vol. 93 (January), edited by Karl Kelsey, 211–24. Philadelphia: University of Pennsylvania.

"The Proper Sieve for Immigrants." 1891. *The Nation,* 5 January, 312.

"School Gunman Reportedly Hated Vietnamese." 1989. *St. Paul Pioneer Press Dispatch,* 19 January, 1A.

Solorzano, Lucia. 1984. "A Second Look at Bilingual Education." *U.S. News and World Report,* 21 June, 24–25.

Stoddard, Lothrop. 1920. *The Rising Tide of Color.* New York: Blue Ribbon Books.

———. 1921. "The Japanese Question in California." In *Present-Day Immigration with Special Reference to the Japanese. The Annals of the American Academy of Political and Social Science,* vol. 93 (January), edited by Karl Kelsey, 42–47. Philadelphia: University of Pennsylvania.

Symms, Steven D. 1985. *Congressional Record,* 99th Cong. 1st Sess. Vol. 131, 22 January, S515–19.

Thomas, Jo. 1980. "Miami Area Divided Over Ballot Proposal to Drop Spanish as a Second Official Language." *New York Times,* 2 November, I, 26.

Truman, Harry S. 1955. *Memoirs.* Vol. 1. Garden City, N.Y.: Doubleday.

Vidal, Gore. 1988. *Armageddon? Essays, 1983–1987.* New York: Random House.

Wright, Guy. 1983a. "Speaking English." *San Francisco Chronicle,* 28 March, n.p.

———. 1983b. "U.S. English." *San Francisco Chronicle,* 20 March, B9.

4 The Federal English Language Amendment: Prospects and Perils

Elliot L. Judd
University of Illinois at Chicago

On April 27, 1981, Senator S. I. Hayakawa of California proposed an amendment to the U.S. Constitution declaring that English be made the "official language" of the United States (Marshall 1986). Since that time, in every congressional session, similar resolutions have been introduced in both houses. None has been passed or even voted upon, and the likelihood of passage of an English Language Amendment (ELA) at the federal level is remote. That is not to say that the ELA is of little importance. It has affected the United States in two important ways. First, it has encouraged the proposal for, and in many cases the enactment of, state and municipal versions of the ELA, which declare English to be the official language and, in some instances, restrict the use of non-English languages. In addition, it has opened up a loud and general debate not just about English and other languages in the United States but about immigration policy, racism, educational policy, and civil liberties.

This essay will focus on the following areas. It will begin with a presentation of the federal ELA as it existed in the 100th Congress (1987–88). The arguments by proponents of the ELA will be listed and then countered. Next, there will be an examination of who the supporters of the ELA are and the possible reasons for their support of the legislation. The paper will conclude with some remarks on the dangers involved in the unlikely event that the ELA should ever become an amendment to the U.S. Constitution.

The ELA in the 100th Congress

During the 100th Congress (1987–88), six ELA measures were introduced. One was a Senate bill (Senate Joint Resolution 13) and the other five were bills in the House of Representatives (House Joint Resolutions 13, 33, 83, and 656 and House Concurrent Resolution 129). They can be classified into two categories, a proscriptive version and a generalized one. The more specific, proscriptive versions read:

> *Section 1*—The English language shall be the official language in the United States.
>
> *Section 2*—Neither the United States nor any State shall require by law, ordinance, regulation, order, decree, program, or policy, the use in the United States of America of any language other than English.
>
> *Section 3*—This article shall not prohibit any law, ordinance, regulation, order, decree, program, or policy requiring educational instruction in a language other than English for the purpose of making students who use a language other than English proficient in English.
>
> *Section 4*—The Congress and the States may enforce this article by appropriate legislation.

The more generalized versions read:

> *Section 1*—The English language shall be the official language of the United States.
>
> *Section 2*—The Congress shall have the power to enforce this article by appropriate legislation.

The two versions are not as different as they appear. Both give the Congress wide latitude to determine what is necessary to implement the "officialness" of English and never specify any limits. While the former version establishes the possibility of using the native language in educational programs designed to make students proficient in English (e.g., transitional bilingual education), the latter could also permit such use even though it is not clearly mentioned. The more detailed form also mentions "the states" enacting English-only measures, although such a wording is really unimportant since this constitutional amendment would supersede any contradictory state laws. Thus, the two versions differ more on surface appearance than in substance.

Proponents of ELA legislation claim that the bills would not outlaw foreign language instruction, the use of non-English languages for public safety and health, or private use of non-English languages by civic groups, ethnic organizations and individuals (Shumway 1987; Symms 1987a, 1987b), but this assurance can be challenged. No guarantee of such protection is provided in the language of either proposed constitutional amendment. Anything not specifically stated in law is open to interpretation, so the enforcement provisions could lead to bans on the use of non-English languages in any of the activities mentioned above. Whether such bans would be declared unconstitutional (e.g., violating the rights to freedom of congregation, speech, religion, etc.) is also an open question. Should the ELA pass as a constitutional amendment, it might be in conflict with other existing amendments, and only the federal courts could rule on which takes precedence. Certainly *without* an ELA, it is unlikely that such prohibitions would be held legally valid (Dale cited in *ELA, 1984*; and Judd 1987, 1989).

Why Pass the ELA: Arguments For and Against

Supporters of the ELA have presented several arguments for why such legislation is needed. They claim that the English language is a symbol of national unity and that it is incumbent of those immigrating to or living in the United States to learn the language. It is argued that English has been a traditional source of stability in the United States, and that in order for social, political, and economic stability to be maintained, people must undergo cultural and linguistic assimilation. Proponents argue that laws and policies that allow the use of non-English languages encourage cultural diversity and fail to force people to learn English. Such multilingualism has allegedly caused monolingual English speakers to be denied jobs and feel like strangers in their own country. Furthermore, because some current government regulations and statutes permit the use of non-English languages, non-English speakers do not bother to learn the common language and thus cannot advance socially or economically. Thus, the claim is that both monolingual English users and non-English users are harmed by such policies (Broomfield 1987a; Shumway 1987; Symms 1987a, 1987b).

Such arguments are based on distortions, misconceptions, and half-truths. First of all, it should be remembered that the framers of the Constitution felt no need to make English the official language even though the country consisted of speakers of many languages (Heath 1977). Our history shows that people could become citizens without demonstrating English language knowledge, that vibrant non-English-language communities have flourished in this country, and that, in general, people's loyalty and patriotism have not been equated with the ability to speak English. It has only been during xenophobic periods in U.S. history that English knowledge was linked with patriotism (Leibowitz 1969, 1976). Historically, there is no evidence that using languages other than English has ever caused political fragmentation. The only major rebellion in U.S. history was the Civil War, and that conflict certainly cannot be traced to language issues.

Also dubious is the assumption that groups that prefer cultural pluralism to linguistic and cultural assimilation are somehow different than previous groups who "melted" into the United States. Certainly, many groups, both past and present, have abandoned their ethnic cultures and languages. However, others have not, either by choice (for example, the Amish or Louisianan French) or as an act of resistance to the larger society (for example, Spanish- or Native Americans). At best, we can say that the melting has varied depending on the group under analysis, the historical period, the location of settlement, the feelings that the group held toward the dominant American society, the receptiveness of the wider society, and a host of other factors (Fishman et al. 1966; Kloss 1977). Equally important is the assumption that retention of ethnic languages and cultures leads to feelings of separatism, antagonism, or disloyalty. No such causality has ever been proven, and to imply such a connection slanders many of us whose parents, grandparents, or other ancestors came to this country and may never have fully mastered the English language. It also disparages the memory of those bilinguals who have died defending this country in numerous wars. In short, statements relating to either monolingualism or cultural/linguistic assimilation as forces for American political stability are either misinformed representations of historical reality or conscious attempts to distort that reality. Are monolingual English users discriminated against in job hiring or made to feel like strangers in their own communities? In some cases, the answer to both may be "yes." In the case of employment, it seems likely that there are few actual instances. Proponents of ELA readily allude to such cases (Symms 1987b), but provide no numbers, just a series of isolated cases. Most of the individual cases cited have occurred in areas where there are large bilingual communities (Miami is the favorite target) and one can argue that the bilingual ability probably is necessary for effective communication with the clients and customers. If such is the case, then such ability is one requisite for the job, and people lacking in this skill would be less than qualified for the position, as would a person who is lacking in other crucial skills. If, on the other hand, such language skills are not required, then discrimination exists and should be redressed in much the same way as in cases of discrimination when English ability is unnecessary for a position. Since ELA advocates never furnish the particulars of these situations, nor list the frequency of occurrence, one is left to speculate on the validity of the charges or whether the omission of the particulars is purposeful or coincidental.

As to whether or not monolingual English users feel alienated in the United States, the ELA supporters provide mostly anecdotes. To be sure, some people feel threatened and uncomfortable in situations where English is the minority language. Historically such situations have always existed in our urban ghettos and isolated rural enclaves. Yet, English has remained the dominant language in American society. There is no danger of its demise in favor of another language, and evidence points to the fact that contemporary immigrants are learning English at the same rate as (or faster than) previous generations. To say that people feel uncomfortable when they do not speak a given language is a natural statement; however, to imply that such a situation threatens the United States or is some form of historical aberration is simply an untruth which provokes suspicion and hatred of non-English users.

Proponents of the ELA often make reference to multilingual situations in other countries to justify the need for an English-only policy in the United States. Pointing to situations in nations like Canada, Belgium, and Sri Lanka, ELA advocates claim that multilingualism is the cause of ethnic antagonism, separatist movements, and political and social fragmentation (Bereuter 1987; Broomfield 1987a, 1987b; Symms 1987a, 1987b). Such a situation will likely occur in the United States unless English is made the sole official language, it is argued.

Drawing analogies from multilingual countries is a dubious line of reasoning. Certainly, there are countries where linguistic issues have been a focus for separatist movements and a factor in political disunity. It is equally easy to find multilingual countries, such as Switzerland or Sweden, that are politically stable. There are also monolingual countries—in Central America and Northern Ireland—that are experiencing similar forms of political instability though language use is not an issue. Do language issues *cause* such civil unrest or are they manifestations of wider feelings of unequal status within a political or economic system?

Further it can be shown that attempts at linguistic repression, where groups are banned from using their ethnic languages, cause feelings of resentment and endanger the system's political stability (for example, Basques in Spain or a variety of ethnic groups in the Soviet Union). What leads anyone to believe that groups whose linguistic freedoms are denied will feel loyal to the government that has repressed them? It should be clear that drawing parallels with certain other countries is a highly unreliable activity. Such a process merely handpicks favored examples, while ignoring parallel situations that may be equally valid.

One policy that ELA proponents particularly decry is bilingual education. They argue that it promotes positive feelings toward the child's ethnic group and home-language at the expense of English. Children fail to learn English, encounter academic failure, leave school, and thus become societal burdens. At best, bilingual education should be used only until the child learns enough English to be mainstreamed into English-only classes and is often totally unnecessary since other educational practices are more successful (Broomfield 1978a; Symms 1987a and 1987b).

These arguments are easily refuted. First, the studies used to fault bilingual education (Baker and de Kanter 1983; Danoff 1978) have been criticized both in terms of their findings and methodology (Cummins 1986; Hakuta 1986; Troike 1978). Some bilingual programs have been poorly run; others have proven successful. Second, federally funded bilingual programs have always had a transitional philosophy that espouses mainstreaming of children, not language maintenance. Finally, can it be proven that children who meet with failure in schools do so because of bilingual education or because of other factors? Is the cause language instruction or malnutrition, poverty, family problems, drugs and/or the numerous other ills that afflict the poor? Would these problems be eliminated by monolingual education? Were dropout rates lower for previous generations who had only monolingual education? Would the situation be better or worse without bilingual education? What we see is a series of unproven arguments presented by ELA advocates. Such arguments ignore the complex issues of education in a pluralistic society and distort reality in favor of a simplistic solution.

ELA supporters have also strongly opposed bilingual ballots. They claim that a person needs to comprehend English in order to make informed electoral decisions. Furthermore, limited English users are supposedly vulnerable to manipulation from unscrupulous forces who bias arguments by only presenting one side in the native language. On the other hand, those knowledgeable in English can select their sources of information and be better informed voters. ELA supporters argue that if one can vote without using English, as well as obtain other services in English such as getting a driver's license, then there is no incentive to learn the language since these services are already available without it (Symms 1987b).

Such arguments may be appealing to a public worried by immigration, but they make little sense. First, it must be remembered that bilingual ballots were introduced to expose people to electoral issues in a language they can grasp. Information is information, regardless of the medium used to convey it. Thus, bilingual materials lead to more— not less—informed voters. Second, there is no evidence of any misuse of bilingual ballots. In fact, it is much easier to find historical examples of voter manipulation among those who *did* fully comprehend English.

Certainly, the problems of uninformed voters manipulated by precinct chapters or clever advertisements is an issue in the United States, but it is not a problem limited to non-English speakers. There is no evidence that those who vote bilingually are any less (or more) informed than their monolingual counterparts.

Who Supports the ELA?

Senate Joint Resolution 13, the Senate version of the ELA in the 100th Congress, was originally cosponsored by seven Senators: Symms, Cochran, Zorinsky, Helms, Thurmond, Garn, and Hatch. However, by the end of the session, there were only five supporters (all Republicans) since Zorinsky had died and his successor did not support the ELA, and Hatch withdrew his cosponsorship later in the session. This represents a decline in Senate ELA support from the previous Congress, where there were 15 sponsors. In the House of Representatives, there were 72 cosponsors of the six ELA measures. Sixty were Republicans and twelve were Democrats. Unlike the Senate, this House support represented an increase from 50 Representatives in the previous session.

In reviewing the list of supporters, it is apparent that the bill attracts legislators who are very conservative and antiliberal. This is not only true in general, but also in comparison with fellow party members. The five Senate Republicans average ADA rating (the most widely used "liberal quotient") was 2 percent and their ACU rating (the parallel conservative rating) averaged 96.8 percent, compared with the 20 percent ADA and 73.4 percent ACU for all Senate Republicans. The same is true in the House, where ELA Republicans averaged 10.2 percent on their ADA ratings (overall Republicans were 20.8 percent) and 92.5 percent on the ACU ratings (as opposed to 80.6 percent for all Republicans). Democratic ELA supporters in the House were even more at odds with their counterparts, averaging 43.2 percent on their ADA ratings (as opposed to 75.2 percent for the average Democrat) and 51.6 percent on their ACU ratings (in contrast to 17.8 percent for all Democrats).

Why does the ELA attract the support it does? It seems many current conservatives are extremely distressed with the social, political, and economic situation in the United States and espouse a return to an America where life was less complex, people were more overtly patriotic, the family was a more cohesive unit, and everyone believed in the same things. It does not matter whether such an America ever existed; it is a nostalgic view that appeals to many people. In today's society, where life has become more complicated, the appeal to simplicity is more attractive than accepting and tackling the reality we face. Foreigners become scapegoats (as they often have in the past) and are blamed for society's problems—loss of jobs to foreign competitors, unemployment, creation of special programs in society that rob taxpayers of their money, rising crime rates, poor schools, illiteracy, and so on.

The ELA fits naturally into this view. Non-English users, and their supporters, are part of these problems. They demand special privileges that others do not receive. They advocate rights not accorded to previous groups. They threaten the very social fabric of society. Rather than address the complex problems in society, it is easier to blame the victims. It is *their* fault because they have not learned English and only measures like the ELA will solve the problem. Once people learn English, all these difficulties will disappear.

It should be noted that the ELA can actually be troublesome to some who hold traditional conservative values. First, it represents direct governmental intrusion into individual rights, an anathema to many conservatives. Classic conservative doctrine holds that the federal government should refrain from intervening in the personal lives and behavior of individuals, and that states and municipalities should be accorded local autonomy. A federal ELA would violate this principle by declaring a national official language and imposing regulations on states and individuals to enforce this provision. Second, for those who believe in the doctrine of "original intent," it is well documented that the framers of the Constitution believed that no official language should be imposed, and the ELA would directly contradict this intent. Thus, the ELA only represents a position of neoconservatives, not traditional ones.

Certainly, the ELA is unattractive to liberals. Many of the policies that are objectionable to ELA supporters are those that have been championed by liberals. They were passed in the belief that it is the role of the federal government to intervene to protect the rights of individuals and groups that have not been accorded equal opportunity. In fact, many liberals feel that should the ELA pass, individual freedoms would be abridged or denied to those who are limited-English speakers. Since the ELA, as a constitutional amendment, would represent the highest law of the land, and since the legislation is so vaguely worded as to allow the banning of any non-English use, it is feared that the ELA could deny basic human rights to many in our society.

Conclusion

There is little likelihood that the ELA will pass in Congress in the near future. Senate support is very weak and House support, while growing, is nowhere near the number required to pass a constitutional amendment. Recent elections give no indication of growing support in Congress, and short of a major political shift, the votes needed to legislate the ELA simply do not exist.

If this is so, why worry about the ELA? The answer is that merely having such bills before Congress has fostered a climate that perpetuates anti-immigrant attitudes and behavior in our society. Many states and municipalities have now passed their own versions of the ELA, obviously spurred on by the movement at the national level. Limited-English users and those who are proficient in English but choose also to use non-English languages are slandered and deprived of rights. The entire country suffers as long as we seriously consider this type of legislation. The ELA poses a threat to freedom in our pluralistic society, and it should be opposed by conservatives and liberals alike.

Works Cited

Baker, K., and A. de Kanter, eds. 1983. *Bilingual Education: A Reappraisal of Federal Policy*. Lexington, Mass.: D.C. Heath.

Bereuter, D. K. 1987. Statement of Representative Bereuter. *Congressional Record* (Washington, D.C.) 133, Daily Edition, 17 December, E4863.

Broomfield, W. S. 1987a. Statement of Representative Broomfield. *Congressional Record* (Washington, D.C.) 133, Daily Edition, 7 January, E43–E44.

_____. 1987b. Statement of Representative Broomfield. *Congressional Record* (Washington, D.C.) 133, Daily Edition, 22 April, E1489.

Congressional Quarterly Weekly Report 47, no. 9 (4 March 1989): 484–86.

Cummins, J. 1986. "Empowering Minority Students: A Framework for Intervention." *Harvard Educational Review* 56: 18–36.

Danoff, M. 1978. *Evaluation of the Impact of ESEA Title VII Spanish/English Bilingual Education Programs*. Palo Alto, Ca.: American Institute for Research.

English Language Amendment. 1984: Hearings on S. J. Res. 167 Before the Subcommittee on the Constitution of the Senate Judiciary Committee. 1984. 98th Congress, 2nd Session. Washington, D.C.: U.S. Government Printing Office.

Fishman, J. A., V. C. Nahirny, J. E. Hofman, and R. G. Hayden. 1966. *Language Loyalty in the United States: The Maintenance and Perpetuation of Non-English Mother Tongues by American Ethnic and Religious Groups*. The Hague: Mouton.

Hakuta, K. 1986. *The Mirror of Language: The Debate on Bilingualism*. New York: Basic Books.

Heath, S. 1977. "Our Language Heritage: A Historical Perspective." In *The Language Connection: From the Classroom to the World*, edited by J. K. Phillips, 23–51. Skokie, Ill.: National Textbook.

Judd, E. L. 1987. "The English Language Amendment: A Case Study on Language and Politics." *TESOL Quarterly* 21: 113–35.

———. 1989. "The English-Only Movement and Foreign Language Teaching." Submitted to the *Modern Language Journal*.

Kloss, H. 1977. *The American Bilingual Tradition*. Rowley, Mass.: Newbury House.

Leibowitz, A. 1969. "English Literacy: Legal Sanctions for Discrimination." *Notre Dame Lawyer* 45: 7–67.

———. 1976. "Language and the Law: The Exercise of Political Power through Official Designation of Language." In *Language and Politics*, edited by W. M. O'Barr and J. F. O'Barr, 449–76. The Hague: Mouton.

Marshall, D. 1986. "The Question of an Official Language: Language Rights and the English Language Amendment." *International Journal of the Sociology of Language* 60: 7–75.

Shumway, N. 1987. Statement of Representative Shumway. *Congressional Record* (Washington, D.C.) 133, Daily Edition, 8 January, E126–E127.

Symms, S. D. 1987a. Statement of Senator Symms. *Congressional Record* (Washington, D.C.) 133, Daily Edition, 6 January, S565.

———. 1987b. Statement of Senator Symms. *Congressional Record* (Washington, D.C.) 133, Daily Edition, 4 June, S7615–S7620.

Troike, R. 1978. *Research Evidence for the Effectiveness of Bilingual Education*. Los Angeles: National Dissemination and Assessment Center.

II The Dangers of Official-English Laws

5 In the Aftermath of the ELA: Stripping Language Minorities of Their Rights

Roseann Dueñas Gonzalez
University of Arizona

Few topics provoke as much scholarly and popular attention as the proposed English Language Amendment (ELA). The media keenly follows the progress of state ELA initiatives (StELAs) and national amendments introduced into Congress. Numerous scholarly studies explicate the legislative and political history of the English-only movement (Judd 1987; Marshall 1986) and its potential effects on minority language groups (Marshall and Gonzalez 1990, in press; San Miguel 1986). Other scholars review the faulty logic and xenophobic underpinnings of the most aggressive of the national umbrella organizations of this movement—U.S. English (Gonzalez, Schott, and Vasquez 1988; Judd 1987).

Yet there is a pervasive misconception among scholars, local and national politicians, and community members who concentrate on the impact of state ELAs while underestimating the strident march of U.S. English toward a federal ELA (FELA). StELAs are assumed to be largely symbolic, ultimately having little effect on civil rights legislation given the precedence of past rulings (Stalker 1988; Veltman 1986), and some scholars call the ratification of a constitutional amendment radical and highly improbable (Marshall 1986; Judd, this volume). Operating under these assumptions, ELA opponents myopically focus on the consequences of StELAs to the exclusion of all else.

In the three states that have most recently passed English-only legislation—Arizona, Colorado, and Florida—the ELA is construed as an innocuous, primarily symbolic gesture. Shortly after a StELA was passed in Arizona, the governor publicly announced that state employees should disregard the law until the constitutionality of the amendment was resolved. Arizona's attorney general also stated in a nonbinding opinion that the enactment "does not prohibit the use of languages other than English that are reasonably necessary to facilitate the day-to-day operation of government" (Bass and Carson 1989).

A similar conclusion was reached when both the governor of Colorado and the mayor of Denver issued executive orders stating that bilingual government information should be provided regardless of the newly passed official-English laws (Paulson 1989, A13). Likewise, in Florida, the legislature has taken no steps to pass laws to put the ballot measure into effect. Unwittingly, ELA opponents comfortably rely upon the supremacy of the United States Constitution and federal statutes to protect the constitutional rights of minorities. By deflecting the public's attention from the larger issue, U.S. English leaders have effectively diffused the power of those who could otherwise defeat them. And upon examining the motives of the organization the real threat is apparent.

The Real Agenda

U.S. English has strong motivations for altering the U.S. Constitution and making English the national language. Ostensibly, its purpose is to protect and preserve the English language; in reality, the organization's most vocal concern is purging the government of foreign language use. Beardsmore and Willemyns (1986, 21) have suggested that the ELA is "masking something far more fundamental and that language is being used as a scapegoat." Plainly, it is not the language issue that ultimately drives U.S. English proponents; rather, it is the fear of potential loss of power and status (Marshall and Gonzalez 1990, in press; Fishman 1988). This paranoia is evidenced by the words of John Tanton (1986, 2), founder of U.S. English: "As whites see their power and control over their lives declining, will they simply go into the night? Or will there be an explosion?"

A classic response to this fear is to introduce legislation which would limit the rights of those perceived to be at the root of the problem. Historically, three conditions in the United States have nurtured widespread support for language-restriction movements: (1) war or national crisis (Heath 1981; Higham 1963); (2) massive immigration (Leibowitz 1969); and (3) economic recession (Billington 1964). These movements contribute to a "hegemonic structure which permits the dominance of certain groups or classes and their languages over others (Skutnabb-Kangas and Phillipson 1989, 5) and result in "linguicism," or racism on the basis of language.

English-only proponents exploit the fears currently felt by United States citizens as they encounter economic crisis and an increasingly diverse America. By employing a sophisticated political and legal strategy, U.S. English has succeeded where past language-restriction movements have failed.

This paper argues that if U.S. English makes the English Language Amendment the highest law of the land, the ultimate impact would be to curtail the constitutional rights of language minorities. The recent successes the organization has enjoyed point toward a future in which English is the constitutionally based language of government and law. Adopting a FELA could eviscerate all the progressive civil rights legislation passed in the 1960s and 1970s.

If a FELA is ratified and federal and state legislation protecting minority rights is challenged, the United States Supreme Court may be asked to reinterpret the validity of current legislation. Four federal statutes and their state counterparts advance specific rights that, prior to their enactment, were actively abridged: (1) the Voting Rights Act of 1965 and its 1975 amendments; (2) the Court Interpreters Act of 1978; (3) the Equal Employment Opportunity Act of 1972 (EEOA); and (4) the Bilingual Education Act of 1968 and its 1974 amendments. The constitutional rights that are endangered follow:

- the 4th Amendment rights to confront witnesses, to have assistance of counsel, and to understand the nature of the charges and the proceedings brought by the government against individual citizens;
- the 5th Amendment right to not be deprived of life, liberty, or property without due process of law;
- the 14th Amendment rights to procedural due process and equal application of the law;
- the 15th Amendment right to vote.

Also at risk are the ephemeral rights of equal access to education and to work in an environment free of discrimination. Protected by federal and state statutes, these rights bridge the linguistic gap between limited or non-English-speaking citizens and government agencies. Compensatory remedies prescribed by three statutes—such as bilingual ballots, bilingual education, and interpreters—grant minorities access to otherwise closed institutions.

U.S. English: The Comprehensive Plan

The rights, central to American citizenship, are under siege by the U.S. English offensive. To accomplish this objective, the organization en-

lists three political and legal tactics: changing attitudes, marshalling
state support, and effectively using legal challenges.

Changing Attitudes

U.S. English employs the media to amass state and federal support for
a FELA. Its major tactic is to disseminate negative attitudes about non-
native English speakers and the consequent urgent need for the ELA
(Bikales 1986; Hayakawa 1987). By presenting unsubstantiated myths,
U.S. English creates an illusion of encroachment, thereby instilling fear
and altering individual perceptions and attitudes. Through its newsletters, U.S. English feeds the national media stories that criticize the
use of Spanish operators by AT&T (*U.S. English*, 1988a), and questions
Spanish programming by NBC (*U.S. English*, 1988b). In each selected
state, prior to an election, U.S. English escalates media reporting to "a
press conference a day" (*U.S. English*, 1988c), highlighting the need for
an ELA. Having won, the organization advances to a new state, leaving
behind turmoil and uncertainty about what the new StELA means.

Once U.S. English has raised the ELA issue in a state, captured the
popular vote, and passed a StELA, a clear political signal is sent to
elected officials: that an ELA is what the state and people want. The
attitudes of state senators and congressional representatives are affected once they see their constituents voting *yes* for such a bill. "Opinion polls showing 60 to 90 percent approval rate[s] have not gone
unnoticed by legislators" (Crawford 1989, 53). When these representatives are faced with the issue, it is very likely they will vote with their
constituents, regardless of their personal beliefs.

Marshalling State Support

As U.S. English uses the media to change attitudes, it also musters
state support. It is clear that the organization's leadership understands
the legal process for proposing and ratifying a constitutional amendment. According to the U.S. Constitution, discussion about new provisions may commence when either "two-thirds of both Houses . . .
propose Amendments" or upon "Application of the Legislatures of
two-thirds of the States . . . call[ing for] a [Constitutional] Convention"
(U.S. Constitution, Article V). Either method is equally valid if the
amendment, after proposal by Congress, is "ratified by the Legislatures of three-fourths of the several States, or by Conventions"
(Article V).

In other words, once U.S. English has secured enough state legislatures that either are supporting, are considering, or have passed

StELAs, it will push for a national discussion to examine the possibility of a constitutional ELA. In general, there are two ways in which a constitutional amendment may be proposed: one involves state legislatures calling for a Constitutional Convention and the other entails both Houses advancing a proposal. Only thirty-three state legislatures are needed before both Houses—or those same state legislatures—are able to begin the arduous process of amending the Constitution. Thirty-eight states, only five more than necessary to call for the Constitutional Convention, are needed to ratify the amendment.

Once enough states support ELAs, U.S. English will argue that there is a legislative mandate before Congress and the Senate—a mandate to approve a national ELA. When the ELA is finally before the Houses for ratification, the prior media exposure and StELAs will expedite the process of passing the proposed amendment. U.S. English will argue that debate is unwarranted as the ELA has already been endlessly contested in the states.

Clearly, the organization has carefully chosen the most cost-effective legal strategy for amending the U.S. Constitution. Investing millions of dollars now in state campaigns reduces the long-term financial and logistical burden of arguing its case at the national level. Changing national attitudes toward a FELA is less burdensome if the work is done in a calculated state-by-state campaign. The strategy is to take advantage of current problems such as the economic crisis and the insecurities it generates, so that the actual ramifications of ELAs remain unquestioned.

Effectively Using Legal Challenge

The lax policing of StELAs by English-only proponents is perplexing to those who misjudge its objective. U.S. English chooses not to waste limited time and resources bringing legal challenges in state courts based on properly promulgated StELAs. It is well aware that StELAs pose no threat to language minorities because of the supremacy of federal statutes protecting civil rights (Gonzalez, Vasquez, and Bischel 1989, in press; Judd 1987).

The supremacy clause declares "that all laws made in pursuance of the Constitution . . . under the authority of the United States . . . shall enjoy legal superiority over any conflicting provision of a State constitution or law" (*Black's Law* 1979, 1292). U.S. English, cognizant of the supremacy argument, predicates its political strategy on this principle. Requisite to making any significant changes in the current body of law,

U.S. English must persuade the American people to enact a constitutional amendment proclaiming English as the official language.

After passage of a FELA, the next step is to challenge the validity of any federal laws contrary to the amendment. An example of a law potentially in conflict with the ELA is the Civil Rights Act of 1964, amended in 1975 to guard voting rights through the use of bilingual ballots. The legal question centers on whether or not the use of bilingual ballots erodes the primacy of the English language. The ultraconservative United States Supreme Court would then consider which of the competing interests requires greater protection—the supremacy of English as the official language or the use of bilingual ballots. If the Supreme Court upholds the supremacy of English, language minorities would, in effect, be denied the right to vote. Finally, once the FELA is enacted, and its validity is borne out by the United States Supreme Court, federal laws contrary to its stated intent are voidable. To void such a law, its constitutionality must first be challenged. Following its efficient strategy, U.S. English need only bring challenges against a handful of federal statutes.

If these federal statues are found to be unconstitutional, a domino effect would then ensue, and any corresponding state laws would become potentially voidable. Given constitutional precedent, challenges to similar state statutes, like those protecting voting rights, would become pro forma and nullification would be inevitable.

Update: The Comprehensive Plan

U.S. English has pursued a manipulative campaign to make English the official language of the United States, and at all levels this calculated plan has advanced its long-term objectives. This organization's concerted effort to change the way the public and lawmakers view the role of English in the United States has convinced many voters that the ELA movement is harmless, that "people wouldn't be required to give up their own language or culture—they would only be required to learn English" (Bramblett 1987, 6A).

One consequence of the uncritical acceptance of U.S. English's platform has been increased reprimands or firings of Spanish speakers by employers who confidently prohibit employees from speaking any language but English on the job (*Gutierrez v. Municipal Court* 1987; Knight and Duarte 1987; Paulson 1989).

U.S. English has surpassed its own timetable for garnering state support. ELA legislation has been introduced in 29 states and passed in 17 (*EPIC Events*, 1989): it has prevailed in over one-half of the 33 states needed to call a Constitutional Convention. In proposing the fifth FELA before Congress, Representative Shumway (1989) touted the number of StELAs as "further evidence of growing support for the English Language Amendment" (4).

In addition to the achievements in its use of the media and in winning elections, the organization intentionally modifies the wording of state ELAs to conform to the political inclinations of the targeted state. Although in Florida English was merely proclaimed the official language, in Arizona a much more restrictive amendment was enacted (*U.S. English*, 1988c). Similar developments have also occurred on the federal level; since 1981 there have been five attempts to introduce a FELA in Congress, each one disparately worded (Marshall 1986; Shumway 1989).

The willingness of U.S. English to pass variously worded amendments indicates adherence to a political strategy that supports its major objective. Not concerned with bringing state-level challenges, it patiently assembles the necessary support in Congress to amend the U.S. Constitution.

The Aftermath of the ELA: A Scenario

Let us consider the effect of the passage of the ELA in one particular state. Like many other states, Arizona relies on both state and federal laws to protect civil rights of minorities. Because Arizona's legal status typifies that of many other states, it epitomizes what might happen across the nation.

Voting Rights

Language minorities in Arizona depend entirely on voting rights protection through virtue of federal law (Gonzalez, Vasquez, and Bischel 1989, in press). Abrogation of the Voting Rights Amendments of 1975, which prohibit the use of English-only ballots, will halt the significant gains made in Hispanic voter registration, a 44 percent increase from 1976 to 1980 in the five southwestern states (Downing 1981). The state would regress to the status quo before 1975 when ballots were printed only in English, literacy tests were pervasive, and voting participation among minorities was extremely low. Although U.S. English conspires to eradicate ethnic voting blocs by abolishing the use of bilingual ballots, rescinding them would all but guarantee an uninformed electorate voting in the very patterns it fears.

Not only will Hispanics be affected, but other language minority groups such as the Navajo will be denied bilingual ballots as well. The invalidation of access rights once enjoyed may, as Marshall and Gonzalez (1990) warn, provoke a sense of frustration impelling these groups to seek redress outside of the political process and perhaps even turn to violence.

Bilingual Education

Bilingual education in Arizona, "permitted" by state law (Ovando and Collier 1985), would become null and void upon a supremacy clause challenge. More than 60 percent of the entire state school-age population in urban centers—limited, non-English-speaking, and linguistically and culturally diverse children—will be affected. An era will commence where children are linguistically restricted and psychologically punished for speaking their native language in school. Furthermore, teachers will no longer have the option to offer linguistically different children a breadth of educational alternatives, and it is probable that these children will be retained in "special" remedial first-grade classes for two to three years and placed in special education courses because language problems will be rampant and unchecked.

The only method allowable under the ELA proponents' scenario to handle the language needs of these limited and non-English-speaking populations would be traditional ESL classes, a method of questionable benefit to American minority children (Task Force 1986). Without bilingual education the learning of content is delayed. And while the language minority child strives to acquire English proficiency, important windows of cognitive opportunity will be missed. Without using the child's native language for instruction, the ability of minority children to keep pace with their English language peers in terms of content will be severely impaired (Wong-Flllmore and Valadez 1986).

Employment Access

After an ELA becomes official, acts of discrimination on the basis of language could be perpetrated against non-English-speaking employees, leaving them no recourse as is currently possible through both federal and state EEOA laws. These acts of discrimination would be completely lawful under a national ELA. For example, in light of the supremacy of the ELA, the discriminatory treatment of bilingual employees could be permissible. Hence, minority language members in the state of Arizona would suffer unchecked racism perpetuated by employers, ignored by government, and sanctioned by the courts.

If the EEOA were declared unconstitutional, no legal remedy would be available in state or federal courts for limited- or non-English-speaking employees. For example, in a 1986 9th Circuit case, a bilingual employee named Gutierrez was restricted from speaking Spanish during breaks and working hours (*Gutierrez v. Municipal Court*, 1987). Relying on the EEOA, the court ruled in favor of Gutierrez because the StELA and the employer's rules were subordinate to federal law. Without an EEOA, language, like the color of a person's skin, becomes a signal (Deutsch 1975) to employers who would otherwise be cautious in their treatment of linguistically different employees.

Court Interpretation

Arizona citizens trust the federal Court Interpreters Act of 1978 to protect their procedural and substantive due process rights. Upon enactment of an ELA, these protections would be lost. The state would return to a time when language minorities were routinely denied due process and equal protection under the law because of their "inability to communicate . . ." and the lack of or the rendering of "poor interpretation . . ." (U.S. Commission 1970).

Gone would be access to fair and equal treatment in the legal system as guaranteed by 5th and 6th Amendment rights: (1) to understand the nature of proceedings, (2) to confront witnesses, and (3) to have assistance of counsel. Qualified court interpreters would no longer be available to any language minority populations.

In Arizona state courts, the use of interpreters has just begun to improve the quality of justice afforded limited- and non-English speakers. The passage of a FELA destroys the impetus to hire interpreters in state courts.

Regardless of U.S. English's alleged intent, this scenario represents one very likely outcome of passing a FELA. Amending the Constitution would change our society's fundamental conceptions of what is fair in education, the workplace, the courts, and the voting booth. As the Arizona example explicates, the number of rights language minorities enjoy will decrease and, as a consequence, their quality of life will suffer.

Conclusions

If the ELA should one day share the constitutional pages with our rights to speech and due process, twenty-five years of civil rights legislation would be imperiled. Understanding the motivations and strategies of U.S. English makes clear the intentions of this powerful lobbying group: to deprive one group of Americans their rights. Federal and state legislation protects the existing constitutional and ephemeral rights of citizens and does not in any way supplant the primacy of English.

To allow discrimination based upon a relatively immutable characteristic such as gender, race, religion, or language is contrary to the basic tenets of the United States Constitution. Denying rights to speakers of other languages allows for a slow but inevitable encroachment upon the rights of us all.

Works Cited

Bass, J., and S. R. Carson. 1989. "Corbin Interprets English Law, Pleases Both Sides." *The Arizona Daily Star*, 25 January, 1A.

Beardsmore, H. B., and R. Willemyns. 1986. "Comment: Language Rights and Language Policies." *International Journal of the Sociology of Language* 60: 117–28.

Bikales, G. 1986. "Comment: The Other Side." *International Journal of the Sociology of Language* 60: 77–85.

Billington, R. 1964. *The Protestant Crusade, 1800–1860*. Chicago: Quadrangle.

Black's Law Dictionary. 5th ed. 1979. St. Paul: West Publishing.

Bramblett, S. 1987. "Agree on English." Letter to the Editor. *The Arizona Daily Star*, 29 December, 6A.

Crawford, J. 1989. *Bilingual Education: History, Politics, Theory, and Practice*. Trenton: Crane Publishing.

Deutsch, K. A. 1975. "The Social Significance of Linguistic Conflicts." In *Les etats multilingues*, edited by J. G. Savard and R. Vigneault, 79–91. Quebec: Leval.

Downing, P. M. 1981. "The Voting Rights Act of 1965: Historical and Policy Aspects." Issue Brief No. IB81079, November. Washington, D.C.: Library of Congress.

Fishman, J. A. 1988. " 'English Only': Its Ghosts, Myths, and Dangers." *International Journal of the Sociology of Language* 74: 125–40.

Gonzalez, R. D., A. A. Schott, and V. F. Vasquez. 1988. "The English Language Amendment: Examining Myths." *English Journal* 77: 24–30.

Gonzalez, R. D., V. Vasquez, and J. Bischel. 1990, in press. "Language Rights and Mexican Americans: Much Ado about Nothing." In *Minority Language Rights and Minority Education: European and North American Perspectives*, edited by P. Laramie. Ithaca: Cornell University Western Studies Program.

Gutierrez v. Municipal Court of the Southeast Judicial District, County of Los Angeles. 1987. No. CV 85-2172-RG, slip op. at 1033, 9th Cir. 5 February.

Hayakawa, S. I. 1987. "Make English Official: One Common Language Makes Our Nation Work." *The Executive Educator* 9, no. 1: 36+.

Heath, S. B. 1981. "English in Our Language Heritage." In *Language in the U.S.A.*, edited by A. Ferguson and S. B. Heath, 6–20. Cambridge, Mass.: Cambridge University Press.

Higham, J. 1963. *Strangers in the Land: Patterns of American Nativism, 1860–1925.* New York: Atheneum.

Judd, E. L. 1987. "The English Language Amendment: A Case Study on Language and Politics." *TESOL Quarterly* 21, no. 1: 113–33.

Leibowitz, A. H. 1969. "English Literacy: Legal Sanction for Discrimination." *Notre Dame Lawyer* 45: 7–67.

Knight, S. M., and C. Duarte. 1987. "English-Only is Policy at Downtown Ramada." *The Arizona Daily Star*, 19 November, 1A, 2A.

Marshall, D. F. 1986. "The Question of an Official Language: Language Rights and the English Language Amendment." *International Journal of the Sociology of Language*, 60: 7–75.

Marshall, D. F., and R. D. Gonzalez. 1990, in press. "Una Lingua, Una Patria? Is Monolingualism Beneficial or Harmful for a Nation's Unity?" In *On the English-Only Movement*, edited by D. Brink and K. Adams. Berlin: Mouton de Gruyter.

Mathes, R. J. 1987. "Bilingual Ballots." Letter to the Editor. *The Arizona Daily Star*, 13 December, 2C.

Ovando, C. J., and V. P. Collier. 1985. *Bilingual and ESL Classrooms: Teaching in Multicultural Contexts.* New York: McGraw-Hill.

Paulson, S. K. 1989. "Four Months after Approval, Result of Three States' English Laws is Unclear." *The Arizona Daily Star*, 3 March, A13.

San Miguel, G. 1986. *One Country, One Language: A Historical Sketch of English Language Movements in the United States.* Available from The Tomas Rivera Center, 710 North College Avenue, Claremont, Ca. 91711.

Sansbury, V. L. 1987. "One English for U.S." Letter to the Editor. *The Arizona Daily Star*, 8 December, 10A.

Shumway, Hon. N. [Congressional Representative from California.] 1989. Legislation Designating English as Official Language of United States. *Congressional Record*, (Washington, D.C.) 135, Daily Edition, 4.

Skuttnabb-Kangas, T., and R. Phillipson. 1989. "Wanted: Linguistic Human Rights." ROLIG-papir 44. Roskilde: Roskilde Universitetcenter Linvistgruppen, 5.

Staff. 1989. "Legislative Roundup." *EPIC Events*, January/February, 5.

Staff. 1988a. "Roundup: AT&T, Espanol." *U.S. English Update*, July/August, 1.

_____. 1988b. "Roundup: NBC Produces Spanish Ad." *U.S. English Update*, July/August, 1.

_____. 1988c. "Official English Claims Victory in Three More States." *U.S. English Update*, November/December, 1.

Stalker, J. C. 1988. "Official English or English Only." *English Journal* 77, no. 3 (March): 18–23.

Tanton, J. 1986. Memo to WITAN IV Attendees. Unpublished Manuscript, 10 October.

Task Force on Racism and Bias in the Teaching of English. 1986. *Expanding Opportunities: Academic Success for Culturally and Linguistically Diverse Students.* Urbana: NCTE.

United States Commission on Civil Rights. 1970. *Mexican Americans and the Administration of Justice in the Southwest.* Washington, D.C.: U.S. Government Printing Office.

Veltman, C. 1986. "Comment." *International Journal of the Sociology of Language* 60: 177–81.

Wong-Fillmore, L. W., and C. Valadez. 1986. "Teaching Bilingual Learners." In *Handbook of Research on Teaching,* edited by M. C. Wittrock, 648–85. New York: Macmillan.

6 Official English and the English Profession

James C. Stalker
Michigan State University

The task that I am undertaking here, predicting the effects on the English teaching profession of the adoption of English as the official language of the United States, is very like writing science fiction. I am constructing a future based on the assumption that a particular event in the present will have noticeable and notable consequences. It is, of course, not a new exercise. Others have preceded me in predicting the effects on society of controlling language; the two most famous are probably George Orwell in *1984* and Aldous Huxley in *Brave New World*, both of whom present quite negative views of the consequences of official control of language.

If we can take these novels as indicators of the success of such predictions, we may take heart. Neither of the worlds projected by Orwell and Huxley developed in quite the ways predicted; we do not live, talk, and write in a world controlled by Newspeak, nor do we chant slogans praising our status as Alphas, Betas, or Gammas. It is possible that Orwell and Huxley were simply depressive doomsayers and that their predicted worlds could not have developed. However, it is also possible that the projection of the possible consequences of the state control of language deterred such control, thwarting the realization of the predictions. Because the second possibility exists, I am undertaking this prediction of consequences.

The Null Hypothesis

The easiest consequence to project is that nothing will happen. Proponents of official-English measures often declare that it will simply be reaffirming a condition that already obtains, that we are doing nothing neither more nor less important or far reaching than legislating a state bird or a state flower. English is the common language; to affirm that fact legislatively will not alter anything. Life in our classrooms will go on as usual. In fact, such is not the case. Legislation declaring English as the official language almost always carries with it some stipulation to the effect that the legislature must or may enforce the official status of English. Because of the vagueness of these enabling statements, any laws become possible, including a law which requires all classroom discourse to be conducted in English. Arizona's recently passed constitutional amendment incorporates restrictive language in the amendment itself: "Every statute, ordinance, rule, order, program, policy or employee of the legislative, executive, or judicial branch of government is required to be in, or conduct business in, English only" ("Official English," 1988, 4). As a governmental unit, public school classrooms are thereby restricted to discourse only in English. The use of a foreign language in a foreign language classroom is specifically allowed in the amendment, but thereby specifically disallowed in all other classrooms.

Classrooms that are already manageable only because teachers and students can communicate in two languages will become impossible because neither can use a common language if it is not English. Furthermore, the demand on resources, which are already overstrained, will increase. *Lau v. Nichols* (1974) and the Joiner Decision reaffirm that all citizens of the United States, no matter what their national, ethnic, or linguistic origins might be, have an equal right to public education. Should that education be restricted so that it must occur only in English, we will be obliged, by law, to provide appropriate classes in English to all who want or need them, so that language will not be a barrier to education. Consequently, we will need to provide more classes devoted solely to English-language instruction than we presently do, in order to serve the needs of those adults who will be obliged to learn English to conduct their normal, daily affairs. A study by the Rand Corporation tells us that there are some 40,000 adults in Los Angeles who want to take English classes but who are on waiting lists because classes are not available. Estimates for the total number of adults who will need English classes run as high as 500,000 in California, 170,000 in Texas, 65,000 in Illinois, and 60,000 in New York. Is it possible that these people could sue the state or the federal government because they are being denied equal access to the official language of the United States? It certainly seems possible.

Under English-only legislation, students, whether child or adult, cannot study subjects such as math in the native language, while studying English in another class; they will be obliged to learn English first so that they can then learn math or science or social studies. As a result, we will need to extend the number of years in which children are in school so that we can teach them English before they begin their academic study. Those of us who teach English as a second language in university programs know from years of experience that an adult student who has a high school or undergraduate college education and who has studied English for three to six years will need an additional six to twelve months of intensive English study (twenty to twenty-five hours per week) in order to reach the level of fluency necessary to survive in a classroom in which English is the language of instruction. Children learn language more quickly than adults, but they do not learn instantaneously. There will be a necessary increase in schooling time if English-only legislation is adopted. We must be aware as well that an increase in schooling time may also ensure a larger number of dropouts who can neither do math nor speak English.

English-Only Becomes Standard-English-Only

The focus of discussion here, as in most considerations of English-only legislation, has been on English as opposed to other languages. However, we must consider another aspect of the world we are projecting for the future. Declaring English as our official language will eventually require that we pick one *kind* of English. In other words, official-English legislation will affect native speakers of English as well as Americans whose native language is not English. There is widespread support for official-English legislation among English teachers at all levels. The general assumption seems to be that English is in jeopardy, that it is blighted and about to expire, and that legalizing English will breathe new life into it and ensure that we will all use it with clarity and brilliance hereafter. The underlying assumption appears to be that we will be legalizing *standard* English. Hence, we have a confliction of two worries: (1) that because clerks in stores and restaurants will not be able to talk to us in English, we cannot get what we want, and (2) that even when they do speak English, they will be mangling our language.

The question then becomes not just whether English will be the official language but *which* English will be the official language, a question which will ultimately have to be decided by the courts, yielding a decision which will then dictate the language which will be used in the classroom. As teachers of English, we all assume that we use and teach standard English in our classrooms, but are we certain that we do? Are we certain that the particular dialect that we use will suffice if we are required, by law, to pass a test, oral and written, which demonstrates that we know and use the legally mandated dialect? Assuming that we would not be required to take such a test is foolish. Many states have already adopted legislation requiring teachers to demonstrate competency in the subject areas that they teach. Adding a test which demonstrates knowledge of and the ability to use a particular variety of English designated as the standard variety is quite easy. The Educational Testing Service, the organization which develops and administers the SAT, GRE, MCAT, and other such assessment instruments, administers the Test of Standard Written English along with the SAT for those who want it. It would be a very small step for a state to require us English teachers to take it as well in order to establish that we are sufficiently competent to teach in English (not just to teach English).

The notion that a state would require its citizens to learn standard English is not a projection into the future. California, the state which often foreshadows events in the rest of the United States, once again leads the way. A bill requiring school systems to determine which students do not use standard English, and to provide remedial work for them, has been introduced in the California legislature several times during the 1980s. It has always been defeated, but the reason given is that the legislature cannot fund the testing and remediation which would be necessary. The defeat has not been on the grounds that we are not sure what standard English is or that variation in native dialect is normal and legitimate and a legislated single dialect is inappropriate. In short, at least one state has already begun the process of legalizing a particular kind of English, a legalization which will inevitably determine the kind of language that teachers and teacher trainers will be obliged to teach and to use in the classroom. The consequences of such a requirement may seem minimal, but in fact such legislation raises old and difficult problems and practices, some of which we thought we were on the road to solving or eliminating. One likely immediate result is that a significant portion of our curricular time will again be devoted to the memorization and testing of usage rules, because these will inevitably be the basis for any definition of standard English adopted by a legislature. It is all that they know. It is what we English teachers taught them.

If we in fact decide that our official English is to be defined as standard English, we must decide whether that standard is to apply to both oral and written English. Are we going to require the non-native speakers of English and the native, but nonstandard, speakers to demonstrate proficiency only in standard, edited, written American English, or will they need to speak it too? If the latter, we must then decide which kind or kinds of spoken English we will legally accept as our standard, our pedagogical target. As difficult as it will be to decide which features define standard, edited, written American English, that decision will be quite an easy task compared with making that determination for spoken English. Because they are socially nonprestigious and have thereby been classified as nonstandard, we can eliminate black English vernacular, Appalachian ("hillbilly"), and the various Hispanic influenced dialects from contention. But we must decide which regional variety or varieties of English will be acceptable. Shall we accept all regional varieties as standard? If so, does that include Appalachian dialect? Are we going to accept all varieties of all regional dialects, working-class through white-collar, or limit standard to the educated varieties of all regional dialects? What level of education then? High school diploma? Bachelor's degree? Master's? Doctorate? Will having achieved these certificates ensure that we are legally using the official standard, or will we be obliged to take a test? Who will make up the test?

By this time, many readers will be responding vehemently to this list of questions. How absurd! Everyone knows what standard English is! And besides, we do not need to legislate standard English just because we have adopted legislation which specifies that English is our official language. But, be aware, we must make these decisions because we have taken the step of legalizing English; hence we must in turn legalize some particular kind or kinds of English, otherwise all varieties of English of whatever kind will be legally English. Indian, or Nigerian, or Filipino, or Australian English will legally be as acceptable as educated Alabaman or working-class Chicago English.

We are a litigious society. The limitations on our daily conduct are increasingly being defined in the courts. The question of the validity or value of such definitions is beside the point here. That it happens is very much to the point. Legal limitations and definitions may take time in coming, but when the first step is taken down the road of legalization, they come. Based on the English-only amendment, legal challenges to the right of municipal employees to use their native language in a public place when that language is not English have been raised in California. Store clerks in Florida are being fired for talking in languages other than English ("Official English," 1988, 1). These actions may seem remote to some of us now, but eventually such actions will affect us personally. If we adopt an "English-only" policy, and then take the next step to "standard-English-only" policy, it is within the realm of possibility that parents or students can sue us for using a nonofficial, nonstandard variety of English in our classroom. Our classroom is, after all, a public place, thereby subject to the dictates of the laws regarding the use of English.

Rejection and Isolation: The Symbolism of English-Only

One of the current buzzwords on university campuses is *internationalization*. Although the word is aesthetically awkward, the concept is certainly appropriate to our time. We are being internationalized whether we like it or not. Our cars, stereos, fax machines, and portable radios come from Japan. Our wine comes from France, Australia, Austria, Spain, Italy, as well as Michigan, New York, and California. Our clothes are made in Hong Kong, Taiwan, Sri Lanka, Mexico. Our Mother's Day bouquets grow in Latin and South America, as do our vegetables. If we ceased being international in our economic life, we would reduce our balance of trade deficits, but we would also reduce our standard of living. We are international in ways that we do not even know. Do you know who owns the mortgage for your condominium or house? It could very easily be a European bank cartel which owns your hometown bank. The intricacies of international finance are nicely illustrated in a recent round of corporate buying. Seagrams, an American company, bought Martell, a French company, but Seagrams is owned by the Bronfmans, a Canadian family ("Let's Make a Deal," 1988, 67). Ford automobiles are manufactured and assembled around the world, and we are all familiar with the burgeoning number of liaisons between Japanese and American companies such as Fuji and Xerox and General Motors and Nissan.

An interesting, and oft highlighted, aspect of this international wheeling and dealing is that the business is conducted in English. When the Japanese sell computer chips to the French, they do so in English. An Italian pilot landing a plane at an Italian airport receives instructions and responds in English. English is the international language, has been for the last century or so, and shows no signs at the moment of losing that function to another language, even those languages which are spoken by larger numbers of native speakers than English, languages such as Spanish and Chinese. Knowing English is an economic asset; not knowing English is an economic hindrance. That is the case within the United States and outside of the United States.

It is easy to conclude from these facts that everyone wants or needs to know English; therefore it is not necessary to learn another language. We would not be able to use it in any case. While realizing that there is some truth in this assertion, we must also realize that not everyone in the world does speak English nor wants to. Part of the not wanting to arises from the same xenophobia which lies behind the English-only legislation. We humans seem to have a natural penchant for staying within our own groups and for regarding outsiders with a great deal of skepticism. That skepticism all too often turns nasty. Lack of knowledge about other people breeds suspicion and rejection of any behavior which is "theirs" as opposed to "ours." Legislation which restricts the possibilities for learning about others encourages the xenophobia which we must guard against if we are to succeed in our contemporary, very international world. Knowing Japanese or German helps us understand the culture that is encoded in the language, and that understanding will enable us to deal with people more effectively, politically, and economically.

Legislation which restricts the classroom use of languages other than English embraces such economically debilitating xenophobia and tells the rest of the world that we are not interested in learning who they really are. Many of these nations, like us, have or want a common language to promote and ensure unity within the country. But that is not really the issue here. We already have a common language. Immigrants to the United States learn English without legal compulsion. Our own marketplace is the best indicator of that; Hispanic radio listeners in Miami desert Spanish-language stations at the rate of five per year ("It's a Whole *Nuevo Mundo*," 1989, 45–46). Given that 68 percent of the available Hispanic audience already listens to English-language stations, it is relatively easy to calculate that, without the support of new immigrants, it will not be long before all Hispanics in Miami are English-only listeners.

Our common language is not in jeopardy. The danger lies not in the loss of English as the common language of the United States, but in the loss of an international view of our role in the world. English-only legislation compels teachers to join in the xenophobia. An English-only viewpoint is an isolationist viewpoint. It reduces other languages to their least communicative and useful function. Because they can only be taught as foreign languages, because they cannot be used in the classroom, or even in the school building, as living communicative languages, they simply become sociolinguistic markers. They function as indicators of a certain level of education, but otherwise they are of no practical use. We arrogantly indicate that we will study certain languages, but that we will not really *learn* them—a rejection and repudiation of all cultures but our own.

The effect of xenophobia on our profession will be the hardest of all to detect. It will be a subtle message we communicate to those who come from other places, children and adults who learn from the classroom that their languages and heritages are things to be ashamed of, the useless baggage of a worthless life. But a worse lesson is the one that we will be teaching ourselves, that our language and our way of life are the only ones of true and real value. To believe that we have a language and culture worth preserving and developing is no crime; to believe that it is the only one worth preserving and developing is self-defeating. English-only legislation encourages us to stick our heads in the sand. It does not encourage us to develop our linguistic resources, along with our other intangible resources, so that we can compete in the international marketplace.

Polarization and Division

Our profession unites us in a common endeavor. We all work at helping our students become literate, educated members of society. We quibble about which authors to teach, whether a product or process approach to teaching writing is more effective, whether to put a period after Ms or not, but despite all of the minor quibbles, we share a common vision and common goals. English-only initiatives strike at the heart of that unity. When we stand in the voting booth to vote for or against an official-English amendment, we can only be for English or against it. At that moment, we become a polarized profession, and the polarization is not of our doing. We are all "for" English; that is why we are English teachers. Yet we are forced to make a decision that is irrelevant to our profession and which divides us rather than joins us so that we can better accomplish our common goals. The consequences for our profession outlined here are negative ones because the official-English initiative is a negative one. Exclusion is a negative act. Orwell and Huxley were right; state control of language implies control on our lives and language, a control which we have never allowed. Our first amendment ensures freedom of speech, freedom to use language as we choose, so long as we do not infringe on the rights of others. In that spirit, we have never established a language academy to codify our language for us. We have never wanted or needed an official language in any form. We still do not.

Works Cited

"It's a Whole *Nuevo Mundo* Out There." 1989. *U.S. News and World Report* 106, no. 9 (15 May): 45–46.

Lau v. Nichols. 1974. 94S. Ct. 786; 414 U.S. 563; 39 L. Ed. 2d I.

"Let's Make a Deal Goes Global." 1988. *U.S. News and World Report* 104, no. 7 (22 February): 66–68.

"Official English Passes in AZ, CO, FL." 1988. *Epic Events* 1, no. 5 (November/ December): 1–4.

III The Deeper Meanings of Language Restrictionism

7 Paranoia in Language Politics

Vivian I. Davis
Eastfield College

In his essay, "The Paranoid Style in American Politics," Richard Hofstadter (1966) traces a phenomenon, not limited to the American political experience, but yet an integral part of it, which develops from the perception that a hostile, conspiratorial world is "directed against a nation, a culture, a way of life" (4). Those who hold this point of view, according to Hofstadter, believe that

> the old American virtues have already been eaten away by cosmopolitans and intellectuals; the old competitive capitalism has been gradually undermined by socialist and communist schemers; the old national security and independence have been destroyed by ... not merely outsiders and foreigners, but ... also ... betrayal at home. (24)

Such a predisposition, Murray Levin (1971) suggests, is not the least un-American, but rather has deep roots in the American culture. He believes that hysteria is whipped up during those times when it serves the interests of big business, politics, and the social elite—that it occurs very seductively in pluralistic trappings, though ultimately it represses true pluralism. Levin believes that this kind of hysteria spreads by cooperation among many elements in the society. Politicians, the media, and a wide range of special interest groups all share the same materials, techniques, and opinions masqueraded as facts, mailing lists, programs, staffs, and finances for widespread and carefully nurtured attacks against chosen targets that seem to them to threaten the "American way." As Levin puts it:

> The deeply felt intolerance that springs from our intense commitment to Americanism, the irrational and impulsive need to defend the assumptions of John Locke and Adam Smith, the anti-Semitism, the nativism, the anti-intellectualism, the vigilantism, the racism, the xenophobia, the pursuit of self-interest under the guise of superpatriotism, and the profound antiradicalism that can be observed "in extremis" during the hysteria have always been

71

and are today the working assumptions of millions of Americans. (1971, 9)

Today it is no longer socially acceptable to be overt or confrontational about such sentiments. It is the style to cloak these feelings in pro-American rhetoric and to enact legislation which indirectly punishes certain groups or ideas. I think we are able to observe these strategies at work in the movement to make English the "official language." Apparently, the languages of current immigrant groups, if not the immigrants themselves, are perceived as threats to the "American way." In the acceptable modern style, we enact legislation to thwart whatever danger these groups and their languages supposedly pose to our traditions.

Two main factors have determined whether the immigrants of a given era are met with hysterical nativism or tolerance: economic need and national self-image. Cyclically, we have welcomed immigrants into the country or shut them out according to prevailing economic conditions. However, white northern Europeans have always been favored over peoples of color, whether they are yellow, red, brown, or black. Immigrants, especially those of color, have always done the least favorable, most dirty, dangerous, dead-end jobs at the lowest wages. As long as immigrant workers can be used to generate quick profits, drive wages down, contain inflation, or to bust unions, Americans have been content to exploit them. But the welcome offered to immigrants is also influenced heavily by the way we perceive our image and security in the world. When we believe America is challenged, we look for scapegoats both inside and outside the country. Immigrants are convenient, they look different, their languages are different. They are outsiders within.

By the mid-1970s, we had lost the war in Vietnam. We had also experienced our first oil crisis, and it was becoming increasingly clear that we were bracing for an economic downturn. Citing particularly the number of Mexicans who were coming back and forth across the border allegedly to take jobs from Americans, President Carter asked Congress to prohibit the hiring of "illegal aliens" and to give legal status to those residing in the United States since 1970. James Cockcroft (1986) traces the history of this movement for the control of our borders which eventually led to the 1982 Simpson-Mazzoli bill. The bill was introduced by Senator Simpson (R-Colorado) as a means of "slamming the door on unwanted Mexican 'wetbacks,' of stemming a potential tidal wave of Caribbean and Central American 'boat people' and 'feet people' and of preserving the nation's culture" (218). As Simpson explained the legislation to his colleagues:

> If language and cultural separatism rise above a certain level, the unity and political stability of the nation will, in time, be seriously eroded. A common language and a core public culture of certain shared values, beliefs and customs make us distinctly "Americans." (222)

Senator Hayakawa (R-California) added a "sense of the Congress" clause to the bill, making English "the official language of the United States." Simpson-Mazzoli did not pass immediately after its introduction, and some believe it was because big business did not think the time was right. Speaker O'Neill said he found no constituency for it when the bill came up in 1983. Eventually Simpson-Mazzoli squeaked through the House of Representatives over the objection of many Mexican-American groups, the Farm Labor Alliance, and the AFL-CIO. The time was starting to be right; Americans felt threatened to the extent that they wanted to limit the number of immigrants, Mexican-Americans in particular, coming into the country.

What changed to make such legislation, as well as the English-only movement, suddenly popular and timely? Here, we must pause to review the litany of events that have created the climate for scapegoating immigrants from Mexico, Central America, the Orient, the Mideast, and Haiti. In the past ten or fifteen years, Americans experienced a runaway budget deficit while the economy went sour and unemployment rose to frightening proportions. Many large United States cities were bankrupt, and homelessness and soup lines, once thought gone forever, had returned. Interest rates were unstable, and young families found it almost impossible to buy homes. The illegal drug trade and the specter of widespread addiction threatened the future of a whole generation, and schools were losing as many students as they were educating. The cost of a college education was becoming an almost unbearable burden for middle-class students. Racial attacks and other violent crimes increased. All these events and others, including the high rate of divorce and family dysfunction, as well as dishonesty in government, disturbed the tranquility of the nation.

Events outside the country were also creating insecurity. Khomeini, who had taken power in Iran, had held American hostages captive for a year in order to punish the United States for having befriended the Shah. The Japanese had begun making and selling phenomenal numbers of cars in the United States, largely because the quality of Japanese cars was superior to that of the American models. Salvadorans and Haitians had fled to the United States in record numbers because life was unbearable under the dictators of both countries. Eventually, the United States assisted both countries in deposing their dictators. Nearly a quarter of a million Cuban boat people had made their way to the United States. And in American schools, the *Lau v. Nichols* ruling was in force, requiring schools to provide remedies for citizens who could not profit from education because they were fluent in languages other than English.

How have all these disparate incidents coalesced in "English-only" sentiment? Hofstadter (1966) explains that many people who consider themselves descendants of "old-family" Americans feel that their ancestors fought for this country, settled it, and made it powerful. For generations their families enjoyed special prestige in America, but today they "feel that they have been pushed out of their rightful place in American life, even out of their neighborhoods" (55). Indeed, it is projected that in the twenty-first century the WASP will be a minority group in America. On the other hand, Hofstadter finds that "new-family" Americans also "have had their peculiar status problem." In the late nineteenth and early twentieth centuries they were the fresh immigrants who had to find a new way of life, a new language, and a new identity while suffering the rebuff of old-family Americans who made them feel inferior and often prevented them from enjoying first-class citizenship rights.

> Status problems take on a special importance in American life because a very large part of the population suffers from one of the most troublesome of all status questions: unable to enjoy the simple luxury of assuming their own nationality as a natural event, they are tormented by a nagging doubt as to whether they are really and truly and fully Americans. (58)

New family descendants must face not only the struggles of everyday life in this complex society where "getting ahead" and "moving up" are the evidences of success, but they must also be able to demonstrate that they are no less patriotic, or loyal, or American than all other Americans. One of the easiest ways to do so is to adopt the American prejudices against certain groups who are mythologized as aliens, deviants, and threats to the American way of life. "Students of prejudice in America have found that patriotism correlates more closely with prejudice than any factor" (Levin 1971, 170). New-family and old-family Americans then are aligned together against current immigrants who are largely from Mexico, Central America, the West Indies, Asia and the Middle East—all peoples of color.

But the situation is more complicated than that. The American population is made up of millions of immigrants and the descendants of millions of immigrants. Many of them still have memories or know stories of hardships in the "old country" where they or their forebears were often political pawns of regimes that had no regard for human rights and where many were too poor to afford the basic necessities—food, clothing and shelter. Their loyalty to the American way of life is not only passionate, but is, from their viewpoint, the least they can give to the land that adopted them and gave them a good life. Consequently, what often appears to others as superpatriotism is something born of their gratitude for having had the good fortune of becoming Americans.

But many Americans are afraid they cannot hang on to what they have and give their children a good start if everyone is allowed to have a piece of the same pie. There is a pervasive fear in this country that material resources are so limited that one group cannot have its basic needs met if all other groups share the same resources. Twenty years ago, Georg Borgstrom (1969), an international food science authority, wrote two books in which he called attention to what he believed was proof that natural resources are dangerously finite:

> Our resources are in most respects, possibly with the temporary exception of energy, grossly inadequate. The gap between the rich and poor nations is widening and threatening within this very century to engulf the few remaining oases. (318)

Borgstrom goes on to make very clear what peoples he believes are a threat to the world's limited resources:

> Has any world politician faced up to the ominous fact that in the year 2000 we will have at least four billion Asians, half a billion Africans, and 600 million Latin Americans? Has any American politician formulated a workable constructive program to cope with a teeming Latin-American world, right at our doorstep, three times as big as the present? The policies of the past have been wholly inadequate. The failure is made glaringly evident by the fact that 100 million Latin Americans, half of the present number, are lacking almost everything—food, homes, water and soil. (318-19)

The philosophy that there is enough in the world, or that enough can be created in the world for all the peoples of the world, does not prevail because as John Dewey observed:

> Civilization existed for most of human history in a state of scarcity in the material basis for a humane life. Our ways of thinking, planning and working have been attuned to this fact. Thanks to science and technology we now live in an age of potential plenty. (Kennedy 1950, 95)

John Dewey may have believed that the potential for plenty exists, and so may a few scientists, but the average American believes Borgstrom's scenario: that the world's goods are scarce and getting more scarce, and therefore, somebody will not make it to the table. Is there any doubt about who the majority of Americans would choose not to invite?

So what has all this to do with making English the "official language" of the United States? A great deal. Such a policy would accomplish everything violence and oppression were once used to achieve—and all legally. Obviously most current immigrants are not now literate in English and likely will not be in the immediate future. How handy to have these new laws which make them illegal, non-citizens, disenfranchised. How convenient, in the name of offering them a chance of assimilation, to actually prevent it. Then these new immigrants will not be able to develop or assert political power and will lack the ability to defend themselves against those groups or laws that would oppress them. They will be unable to compete in the market place; thus they will always be a ready pool of laborers for the dead-end, risky, low-paying jobs that "true" Americans do not want. At the same time they will be easily expendable in the marketplace. If these individuals or groups cannot communicate in the "official" language of the land, they legally will not be able to communicate at all because "officially" they will have said nothing no matter what they say, or how they say it.

Works Cited

Borgstrom, Georg. 1969. *Too Many; A Study of Earth's Biological Limitations.* New York: The Macmillan Company.

Cockcroft, James D. 1986. *Outlaws in the Promised Land: Mexican Immigrant Workers and America's Future.* New York: Grove Press.

Hofstadter, Richard. 1966. *The Paranoid Style in American Politics and Other Essays.* New York: Alfred A. Knopf.

Kennedy, Gail, ed. 1950. *Pragmatism and American Culture: Problems in American Civilization.* Lexington, Mass.: D. C. Heath and Company.

Levin, Murray B. 1971. *Political Hysteria in America: The Democratic Capacity for Repression.* New York: Basic Books.

8 *Solamente Inglés* and Hispanics

Victor Villanueva, Jr.
Northern Arizona University

A colleague speaks of minorities in academics having gotten so much handed them that they don't know their limitations. Did he say "Give 'em an inch and they'll take a mile"? I tell my wife. She says "Do you realize he said 'Give 'em an inch and they'll take a mile'"?

At a restaurant a basic-writing advocate tells of having been effectively conned by a young Puerto Rican. Clever, the things these Puerto Ricans will do to get a buck. A Puerto Rican sat beside her. I do not appear the stereotypical spic.

"Spics" is what we are called. The term is a racial reference with a linguistic history: "No speak English." "No spic." "Spic."

John Tanton's Hispanic hysteria had been exposed. He had founded an organization to support the English Language Amendment because he feared a Hispanic takeover, a takeover by fast-breeders faithful to a Roman Church which does not respect the division of church and state (Ingerson 1988, 5; LaFranchi 1988, 18). He had said that America is going to face "the first instance in which those with their pants up are going to get caught with their pants down" (Wingert 1989). He said all this. Newspapers wrote of how he said this. There were grand gestures: Linda Chavez's resignation; Walter Cronkite's resignation. And still English-only propositions passed in state after state. Tanton, I must believe, was regarded as an aberration, the bad apple, not at the core of the intent of an English Language Amendment.

There must be many who believe that those of us who say English-language legislation is a racial or ethnic matter are overreacting, displaying our typical minority oversensitivity. Advocates of an English Language Amendment must believe that minorities do not understand that the non-English speaker's welfare, as well as the nation's, rests on our mutual ability to communicate through a common tongue. This is a secret to no one.

We know that although a command of English might not guarantee power, its lack pretty well guarantees powerlessness. No one can argue against the primacy of English at this time in history. But one can argue a history of confusing race and language, of official subjugation in the name of unity. America has a history of Tantons and of a historic ill will to Hispanics, to anyone not of western European stock.

In 1907 President Theodore Roosevelt appointed an immigration commission to study what was being perceived of as an immigration problem. By 1911 the commission issued a forty-two-volume report. Its findings were that the new immigrants, eastern and southern Europeans, were inherently inferior to the older immigrants. The commission cited a noted anthropologist, Madison Grant, who wrote,

> The new immigration contained a large and increasing number of the weak, the broken, and the mentally crippled of all races drawn from the lowest stratum of the Mediterranean basin and the Balkans, together with hordes of the wretched, submerged populations of the Polish ghettoes. Our jails, insane asylums, and almshouses are filled with human flotsam and the whole tone of American life, social, moral, and political, has been lowered and vulgarized by them. (Estrada et al. 1981, 115)

Italians are still "ethnic." We still tell Polish jokes.

Mexicans were viewed in even less favorable terms. New Mexico was denied statehood until Anglos outnumbered the Hispanics (Conklin and Lourie 1983). Arizona's bid for statehood at the turn of the century had been denied several times on the basis of its Mexican population, referring to the Mexican "mongrel racial character." In 1924, America closed the doors to free immigration from Europe. The doors had already been closed to Asians in the Chinese Exclusion Act of 1882. Mexicans could work the farms, railroads, and mines but not apply for citizenship. Come in, but go back when the work is done. Then in 1928, during congressional hearings on Western Hemisphere immigration, attempts were made at stopping even this revolving door. The case against Mexicans was summed up by one eloquent speaker to the hearings. As for Mexicans, he said,

> Their minds run to nothing higher than animal functions—eat, sleep, and sexual debauchery. In every huddle of Mexican shacks one meets the same idleness, hordes of hungry dogs, and filthy children with faces plastered with flies, disease, lice, human filth, stench, promiscuous fornication, bastardly, lounging, apathetic peons and lazy squaws, beans and dried fruit, liquor, general squalor, and envy and hatred of the gringo. These people sleep by day and prowl by night like coyotes, stealing anything they can get their hands on, no matter how useless to them it may be. Nothing left outside is safe unless padlocked or chained down. Yet there are Americans clamoring for more of these human swine to be brought over from Mexico. (Estrada et al. 1981, 116)

The swine continued to be brought over as long as there was profit in having them.

But when the profits ran out, the Mexicans were kicked out. When the Great Depression hit, Mexicans and Mexican-Americans who applied for relief were directed to "Mexican Bureaus." The Bureaus' job was to repatriate Mexicans—without regard to citizenship. Like swine, they were stuffed into cattle cars and railroaded to a home that for many had never been theirs. In 1933 a Los Angeles eyewitness to the repatriation process expressed a relatively common sentiment:

> The repatriation programme is regarded locally as a piece of consummate statecraft. The average per family cost of executing it is $71.14, including food and transportation. It cost one Los Angeles County $77,249.29 to repatriate one shipment of 6,024. It would have cost $424,933.70 to provide this number with such charitable assistance as they would have been entitled to had they remained—a savings of $347,468.40. (Estrada et al. 1981, 118)

From 1929-34 the number of repatriated Mexicans exceeded 400,000. Approximately half were native to the United States. We can only speculate on the number who would have been American and Anglicized, educated in American schools, playing with Anglo kids. The immigrants had known English. It was the law.

"But it's English which unites us"

There are no doubt many whose concern really is with providing everyone equal access to America's bounties. Prosperity requires a common language. That language is English. Former Senator Huddleston explained the history to a special subcommittee of the Senate Judiciary Committee on English-language legislation:

> For over 200 years, the United States has enjoyed the blessing of one primary language that is spoken and understood by most of its citizens. The previous unquestioned acceptance of the language by immigrants from every linguistic and cultural background has enabled us to come together and prosper as one people. (1984, 15)

The line between myth and history is being blurred here. America had known hundreds of native languages before Europeans arrived. We know that not all Native Americans passively adopted the languages of the colonizers. The colonists brought Dutch and some Swedish to the New York-Delaware area. The Holland Tunnel remains and

Rutgers University. The Huguenots brought French to Louisiana, an officially bilingual state to this day. The Spaniards brought Spanish to Florida, the Southwest, and the West. Germans brought their language to Pennsylvania. Pennsylvania "Dutch" (really Deutsche) remains a distinct dialect, its German influence still present. I have eaten frank-furters with kraut and mustard since long before *kindergarten*. We are full of German. It is American—not "ethnic," like, say, tacos or Spanish rice.

Germans did not quietly accept the primacy of English. Those who were in America during the Revolutionary War era were in no hurry to learn English. They brought out the Tanton in Benjamin Franklin, who asked, back in 1751,

> Why should the *Palatine Boors* [Germans] be suffered to swarm onto our Settlements and, by herding together, establish their Language and Manners, to the Exclusion of ours? Why should *Pennsylvania*, founded by the *English*, become a Colony of *Aliens*, who will shortly be so numerous as to Germanize us instead of our Anglifying them? (Weaver 1970, 57)

Franklin saw Germans the way Tanton sees Hispanics. But Franklin responded differently. The Founding Fathers figured more unity could be had in pluralism than in subjugation. The Germans would be nec-essary allies in a revolution. Government documents were published in German. After the war, during the drafting of the Constitution, the new nation's designers still decided not to officialize English, despite the perceived threat of a German primacy. The nation builders be-lieved that principles of freedom should include linguistic freedom—even the freedom to speak what the Fathers believed to be an inferior tongue (Heath 1976). German remained America's semi-official second language until this century.

It was a semi-official second language in that there were some in-stances of official German in the United States. In 1795 Germans peti-tioned the new congress to have laws published in German as well as English. The petition of the Virginia delegation made it through com-mittee, falling to defeat by only one vote. In the years between 1830 and 1890 4.5 million more Germans came to the United States. Seven years after the first wave, 1837, Pennsylvania legislated that the public schools be conducted in English and German—legislated that German would have equal status with English. By 1840 Ohio's public schools were bilingual German-English. Some schools in Minnesota, Mary-land, and Indiana were exclusively German (Fallows 1987). Publicly-funded German schools existed through much of the nineteenth cen-tury (Conklin and Lourie 1983).

The schools did not completely die out until the first world war. Then the German-Americans quieted, quickly assimilated (nearly two hundred years after their first arrival). Their ancestry had made them enemies to many here during the war. But since ancestry, not race, was the issue, fluency in English did mark the end to their persecution during the war.

After the first world war the push for "100 percent Americanization" saw bilingual education give way to something like current teachings of English as a second language. Mexican-Americans, along with other minorities, were included in a nationwide push at Americanizing the "immigrant," a push with remarkable similarities to the present day. The California Commission on Immigration and Housing, for example, outwardly declared its endorsement of "Americanization propaganda" (Fallows 1987, 378). The propaganda campaign evidently worked, given Huddleston's common belief in a monolingual American past.

Among those being compelled to Americanize were not only Mexicans but the "new immigrants" as well—the Italians, Yugoslavs, Poles, Rumanians who were living in ghettos. They were the inherently inferior, said the anthropologist and public sentiment. The public believed they were refusing to learn English (Hakuta 1987). Already forgotten was the bona fide, documented, legislated German refusal.

Intensive English instruction was mandated and instituted. Penalties were imposed on those who spoke other languages. Successful learning of English was gauged by students' abilities to speak like the Anglo middle class. The success of these programs was measured by standardized achievement tests and I.Q. tests, just as successes are measured today. These and other criteria determined students' high school curricula, with racial minorities and immigrants consistently finding their ways into trade-oriented schools rather than college preparatory schools.

By the 1930s English oral proficiency had become a precondition for immigration. English literacy had become a precondition for voting, a requirement also aimed at southern Blacks—who were neither immigrants nor bilingual. Language-as-unifier has been used to exclude before.

"But there are cities where no English can be heard"

We hear that today there are many Spanish-speaking ghettos, that the difference between the "new immigrants" of the twenties and the Hispanics of today is a matter of numbers. This is so. But it reflects an earlier wave of assimilation. And it reflects American history. Hispanics are only partly the descendants of Spain; we are also descendants of the indigenous peoples of these lands before the Spaniards and (at least for the Caribbean Hispanic) of the West Africans who came to this continent as slaves. Only Native Americans have been on this continent longer than the descendants of Spain.

Apart from what is now the Pacific Northwest, Florida and all the land west of the Mississippi were once claimed by Mexico or Spain. Hispanic immigrants are many, but so too are Hispanic citizens, natives to the lands of the United States. The New World belonged to Spain, claimed by Columbus (an Italian, one of the inherently inferior, the European founder of the continent named after another Italian. History is apparently stored in short-term memory). Columbus was "Colon" to the Spaniards. Colon is still a common surname among Caribbean Hispanics. In 1513 Ponce de Leon discovered Florida. In 1565 the Spaniards established their first colony in St. Augustine. By 1540 Francisco Vazquez de Coronado had conquered the Aztec Empire and explored what is now Arizona, Texas, Colorado, and New Mexico. In 1598 Juan de Oñate founded Gabriel de los Españoles, the Chamita of New Mexico who still claim a direct lineage to Spain, who still speak Castilian Spanish, the ancient dialect of prestige. In the Caribbean, the Arawak and Boricua languages of Puerto Ricans, the native Indian tongues of Cubans, were erased by the Spaniards. We are many groups united in having been subjected to Spanish-only mandates for four hundred years.

"Hispanic" is a convenience created by the Census Bureau. Mexican, Cuban, and Nicaraguan immigrants might have cultural and linguistic similarities, but they also differ. Puerto Ricans and Mexican-Americans are not even immigrants, a good number of us monolingual in English yet not assimilated in the usual sense.

"Somos blancos," descended from Spain, Mami would say. Mexicans "son Indios," Dad would say. They didn't see the Indi in mi abuela's features. They didn't see the West African in my sister. Like Anglos in America today, Mami and Dad confused race and language.

A bumper sticker reads "Polish and proud of it." I wonder if the driver knows the language. I remember:

> This generation, of which I am a part, never had to face the problem of pulling away from Polonia. We had never properly belonged to it. To us it was a slowly decaying world of aged folks living largely in a dream. One day it would pass and there would remain only Americans whose forebears had once been Poles. (Conklin and Lourie 1983, 1)

Despite the hardships, the new immigrants did assimilate, the Polish joke nearly all that remains of a harsher time. Yet the memory of that harder time still has the new immigrant claiming Polonia, Italia, "the old country." We are alike in some ways, the Polack and the Spic. Writing about United States-born Puerto Ricans, sociolinguist Ana Celia Zentella notes that "today the second generation (which, as of the 1980 Census, accounts for over 50 percent of the total number of Puerto Ricans in the United States) and the uncounted third generation do not know much about the island or its history, nor do most yearn to return, but their situation here is not significantly different from that of their parents or grandparents" (1988, 141). So we become Hispanics, responding to an established pattern. The common threat promotes the common bond.

The numbers of Spanish-speaking ghettos may be great. But the numbers resistant to English-learning are negligible. Ninety-eight percent of Hispanics responding to a national survey conducted in 1985 believed it essential for their children to learn to read and write "perfect" English (Hakuta 1987).

Today I struggle to regain the Spanish I spoke as a child. My sister, thirteen years my younger, is ostensibly third-generation American-born. She cannot even say "no" in Spanish, or so my mother jokes, a sadness to her voice. I struggle to pass the heritage onto my children, while I teach what I know of English, the knowledge of my trade.

English is the global lingua franca. The chairman of the PLO sits, traditional headgear wrapped around his head and draping over combat fatigues, the nationalist, one we call a terrorist. He speaks to a PBS newsman in fluent English. He assumes the language of a journalist; he does not assume the language of a nationalist who regularly draws global attention. PBS television's "The Story of English" notes that an Air Italia commercial jet, flying over Italian airspace, making a routine local run, piloted by Italians, speaking to a ground crew which is exclusively Italian must nevertheless speak in English. If a student in Beijing or Liberia or Mexico City recognizes the need for English, surely the American or would-be American recognizes the need.

We all know that English in America contributes to a national sensibility, can promote unity. But it cannot remedy ethnocentrism and racism. Consider the example of Lauro Cavazos. During the most recent presidential campaign, George Bush announced that if he were elected president he would appoint a Hispanic to his cabinet. A few days later Cavazos became Secretary of Education. The Hispanic community and others thought it nice, even if suspicious, to have a Hispanic in high office. But why was his being a Hispanic so clearly a principal—if not the primary—qualification for the job? We figure to right a wrong, maybe even overcompensate. Yet the focus on his ethnicity seems more a sign of a persisting inequity, that Hispanics cannot be seen as simply Americans, no matter how Americanized, no matter how Anglicized. Cavazos is an English-speaking, sixth-generation Texan, the president of a university. Six generations say he is not an immigrant; they suggest an American ancestry and a U.S. citizenship dating further back than the residence and history of citizenship of one of the most recent presidential candidates. A university president suggests that he is not likely to be one of the handful of Hispanic separatists from two decades ago whom S. I. Hayakawa is fond of citing (Hayakawa 1987). Cavazos cannot get more assimilated. There is no telltale Spanish in his speech. He does not even sport Indian features. He must have met and exceeded all the conditions to becoming an assimilated American. Yet the public still sees a hyphenated American.

More than a half century has passed since the last time language laws sought to exclude a portion of the population. We look back with embarrassment at the not-so-empirical findings of an anthropologist or the not-so-wise words of state officials. Yet we are now again attempting essentially the same policies for essentially the same reasons—Tanton's reasons, if not always by intent but in effect.

Non-English speakers must learn English. But a law suggests punishment. The punishment would be levied almost exclusively at one group of people—as it has in the past. I doubt that those who are concerned with the welfare of the Spanish-speaking minority or immigrant intend to be punitive. Yet there remains the possibility of an English Language Amendment. We deny plurality to reaffirm an ethnocentric and xenophobic past we would like to tell ourselves and the world we have transcended.

Works Cited

Bonilla, F., and R. Campos. 1981. "A Wealth of Poor: Puerto Ricans in the New Economic Order." *Daedalus* 2: 134–76.

Conklin, N. F., and M. A. Lourie. 1983. *A Host of Tongues: Language Communities in the United States.* New York: Free Press.

English Language Amendment, 1984: Hearings on S. J. Res. 167 before the Subcommittee on the Constitution of the Senate Judiciary Committee. 1984. 98th Cong., 2nd Sess. 1284. Washington, D.C.: Government Printing Office.

Estrada, L. F., F. C. Garcia, R. F. Macias, and F. Maldonado. 1981. "Chicanos in the United States: A History of Exploitation and Resistance." *Daedalus* 2: 103–31.

Fallows, J. 1987. "Bilingual Education." In *Crossing Cultures,* edited by H. Knepler and M. Knepler, 378–88. New York: Macmillan.

Hakuta, K. 1987. Public Testimony to the Connecticut State Legislature. 30 March.

Hayakawa, S. I. 1987. "Why English Should Be Our Official Language." *The Educational Digest* 52, no. 9 : 36-37.

Heath, S. B. 1976. "A National Language Academy?: Debate in the New Nation." *International Journal of the Sociology of Language* 11: 9-43.

_____. 1977. "Our Language Heritage: A Historical Perspective." In *The Language Connection: From the Classroom to the World,* edited by J. K. Phillips, 23-51. Skokie, Ill.: National Textbook.

Ingerson, Marshall. 1988. "Push for Official English in Three States." *Christian Science Monitor* 80, no. 233 (27 October): 5.

LaFranchia, Howard. 1988. "Election '88: The Mountain West." *Christian Science Monitor* 80, no. 234 (28 October): 18.

Stalker, J. C. 1987. "Official English or English Only." *English Journal* 77: 18-23.

Wingert, P. 1989. "Say it in English." *Newsweek* 113, no. 8 (20 February): 22-23.

Zentella, A. C. 1988. "The Language Situation of Puerto Ricans." In *Language Diversity: Problem or Resource?* edited by S. L. McKay and S. C. Wong, 140-65. Cambridge, Mass.: Newbury.

9 Anglo-Conformity: Folk Remedy for Lost Hegemony

James Sledd
University of Texas at Austin

"Will America be the death of English?" asked Edwin Newman in 1974—and mournfully answered, "Yes." A few years later, as Paul Copperman, in *The Literacy Hoax* (1980), lamented "the decline of reading, writing, and learning in the public schools," John Simon (1980) praised Newman's "civil tongue" but condemned the citizenry at large as "a nation of wordmongers or word-butchers," whose "abuse of language" would lead "to a deterioration of moral values and standards of living" (58–61).

Not only journalists were convinced that U.S. education was in decay and American English an endangered species among languages. The Educational Testing Service and the College Board alarmed the entire nation with eager reporting and ambiguous analysis of falling scores on the supposed test of scholastic aptitude, whose verbal part has been described by John B. Carroll as "essentially a test of 'advanced vocabulary knowledge' " (Hirsch 1987, 4). The National Commission on Excellence in Education responded to such alarms by announcing that "a rising tide of mediocrity" had put our nation at risk: "The educational foundations of our society are presently being eroded by a rising tide of mediocrity that threatens our very future as a Nation and a people" (National Commission on Excellence in Education 1983). One need not read beyond a single page to learn, from this and similar assertions, that "what was unimaginable a generation ago has begun to occur"—that the subject of the Commission's deliberations has virtually ceased to exist.

In such funereal commentary, the supposedly dying tongue that Shakespeare (mis)spake remained a favorite subject. Though the 1980s began with British professor Geoffrey Leech ("Jolly Good," 1980, 9) affirming that Americans use English more correctly than the Brits, Americans were not persuaded, and both institutional and individual eminences made stern demands on the language of the Republic's

87

citizens and of its guests. In its pamphlet *Academic Preparation for College* (1983), the testy College Board presumed to define "the Basic Academic Competencies," which it called "essential to effective work in all fields of college study" (7–9). Two of those competencies were the abilities to speak and write standard English well. College freshmen who lacked the competencies (as certainly a majority of Americans do) would discover that without them "knowledge of history, science, language, and all other subjects is unattainable." Habitual utterance of *to finalize* would presumably finalize a state of utter ignorance.

The University of Virginia's E. D. Hirsch, Jr., an individual devotee of such testing as has pestered students and teachers throughout the 1980s, set out with two of his colleagues to avert disaster by producing a new kind of dictionary. Believing that the grammar and pronunciation of standard English had already been fixed and frozen, Hirsch made it his task to define "a universally shared national vocabulary . . . a vocabulary that we are able to use throughout the land because we share associations with others in our society." Three Virginia academics, that is, would define "what every American needs to know" and would urge upon the schools the responsibility of conveying to all students the knowledge embodied in their *Dictionary of Cultural Literacy* (Hirsch 1987, 26; Hirsch, Kett, and Trefil 1988).

Hirsch's notions were publicized nationally and gave academics the opportunity to denounce one another even more vigorously than usual, but the preservers and defenders of the English language who got the most publicity and ignited the most numerous quarrels were those who sought by constitutional amendments to make English the sole official language of the nation and its various states. The first of several English Language Amendments to the federal Constitution was proposed as early as 1981 by Canadian-born Senator S. I. Hayakawa of California. His proposal would not only make English "the official language of the United States," it would also forbid both federal and state governments to "make or enforce any law which requires the use of any language other than English" (Marshall 1986, 23–25). The consequences of such an amendment would be hard to calculate, but Hayakawa made it plain that he intended (among other things) to limit bilingual education and to abolish pluralingual ballots.

U.S. English, the organization of which Hayakawa became honorary chair after leaving the Senate, has been more concerned with consequences which allegedly will follow if English is *not* made our official language. The United States, it is commonly suggested, might become "a poly-lingual babel," torn apart by "political upheavals over language" (McClellan 1989, 17). The extent to which promotion of an English Language Amendment has promoted national unity may be judged from the last sentence of a Texan's open letter to Hayakawa: "Promote it in hell, Dr. Hayakawa" (17).

Among the questions which concern about the language raises is that of why this concern itself is so extreme at just the present time. English today is the most successful language in the history of the world, the nearest approach to a *universal* language that has ever been made. In 1977, Andrew W. Conrad and Joshua A. Fishman called English "the primary candidate for a universal international language role." It is, Fishman and Conrad said, "*the* language of diplomacy, the predominate language in which mail is written, the principal language of aviation and of radio broadcasting, the first language of nearly 300 million people, and an additional language of perhaps that many more" (6–7). In 1982 Braj Kachru wrote, "The extent and degree of the spread of English, and its manifestations in various cultures, is unequaled" (9). In 1987, Ronald Wardhaugh found English "spoken almost everywhere in the world to some degree. No other language," Wardhaugh said, "has ever been spread so far and wide. No other language has ever had the influence in world affairs that English has today." Wardhaugh was optimistic about the future as well. "There is also no indication that English is in any way ceasing to spread; indeed it seems to be on the ascen[t] in the world with no serious competitor" (15, 131, 128). Sir Randolph Quirk and his colleagues, in their monumental *Comprehensive Grammar of the English Language* (1985), summed up the unquestioned consensus of linguistic scholars in their first sentence: "English is generally acknowledged to be the world's most important language" (3).

Within the United States, the dominance of English is unquestioned and unquestionable. Representative citizens, almost embarrassingly monolingual, can testify to English dominance in radio, television, film, newspapers, magazines, books, education, business, industry, the armed forces, politics, and government. The evidence of direct experience is backed by the testimony of an alphabet of experts:

> There is no minority language in the United States that can aspire to threaten the position of English as our principal language. Despite the cultural and linguistic diversity in the United States, English will continue to enjoy the primacy it deserves. (Alatis 1986, 198)

> The children of American immigrants soon learn that speaking English is demanded for acceptance by American society. (Cafferty 1980, 2)

> Without either constitutional or subsequent legal declaration or
> requirement that English is the *official* (let alone the *national*) lan-
> guage, a complex web of customs, institutions, and programs has
> long fostered well-nigh exclusive reliance upon English in public
> life. (Fishman 1981, 517)

> In the United States, practically all the important institutions, es-
> pecially those in . . . the domains that control or dictate the lan-
> guage to be used, the language for "success" or aspiration, the
> language of prestige and power—all use English. English is the
> desired language of the immigrant. . . . By force of tradition and
> because of the language in the controlling domains, English will
> "prevail." Immigrants sooner or later . . . will be using English even
> if it is not declared an official language. (Sibayan 1986, 163)

> Although English is not the official language of the United States,
> which has no official language, it is nevertheless the language of
> the Constitution itself and the language that is used almost every-
> where in the country for just about all official purposes. . . . There
> is no doubt that English is de facto if not de jure the official lan-
> guage of the United States." (Wardhaugh 1987, 245)

It is particularly notable that many scholars see bilingual education
as no threat to the dominance of English in the United States. According to Shirley Brice Heath, the Bilingual Education Act (1968) "promoted the use of the mother tongue of language-minority students in the
early elementary years"—but with the ultimate aim of improving their
"academic performance *in English*" (1985, 267; emphasis added). James
Alatis, Kenji Hakuta, and Victoria F. Vasquez (names quite as honora-
bly American as *Heath*) agree that actual programs of bilingual education "are mainly transitional" (Hakuta 1986, 215)—that is, "the aim is
quickly to mainstream the child into an English-dominant classroom"
(Gonzalez, Schott, and Vasquez 1988, 27–28). Alatis puts the case
strongly: "All bilingual programs offered in the United States aim at
English language proficiency as their primary goal. The majority of
students in bilingual programs actually receive more English instruction than do students placed in all-English programs" (1986, 199).

Even maintenance programs (bilingual programs which aim not
just to cultivate proficiency in English but to maintain it in the other
language) may have ironically ambiguous effects, as Noel Epstein of
the *Washington Post* points out: "If such efforts were to succeed, they
would be just as likely to help erode ethnic languages and cultures in
America as to nourish them. As Dr. Fishman comments, research 'has
conclusively demonstrated . . . that the school is a rather unreliable ally
of language maintenance, leading appreciably and frequently in other
directions, i.e., toward the *wider* language of marketplace, of industry,
of government and of scholarship' " (1980, 101). David E. Lopez should

surprise no one, therefore, by his remark that "Spanish and Navaho are the only languages that are passed on from generation to generation to significant degrees. Furthermore, at least in the case of Spanish, passing on Spanish is a minority pattern; after the second generation, English is the dominant language of most Hispanics . . ." (1982b, 40). At least in cities, "the pressure of English" continually operates against the Spanish component of such English-Spanish bilingualism (Lopez 1982a, 46).

The testimony of so many close observers sharpens the question of why the concern about the decline of English and the consequent fracturing of the American Union has been raised at the very moment when English is most successful abroad and quite secure at home. The answer here offered for the reader's consideration and judgment is simple but sweeping. The concern is basically *not about language* and not about an imagined end to national unity *but about hegemony*—the enforcement of "Anglo-conformity" within and of submission to U.S. power without.[1] More succinctly, the concern arises from the fear of the dominant that they may lose their dominance. Threatened by swift, huge change, comfortable people retreat into nostalgia for the good old days which were once the bad new days. Looking for something controllable in a situation apparently beyond control, the threatened turn from the concrete to the symbolic, from things to words. That maneuver has the advantage of providing scape-goats. Changed patterns of immigration into a nation grown insecure have created hostility to the newcomers, especially to the growing minority of Spanish speakers. An English Language Amendment can serve as a warning: this is Anglo country.

For this unoriginal hypothesis, readers sufficiently interested can find considerable support in reputable sources. In a well-known essay, Heath has written, "Throughout the history of the United States, whenever speakers of varieties of English or other languages have been viewed as politically, socially, or economically threatening, their language has become a focus for arguments in favor of both restrictions of their use and imposition of standard English" (1981, 10). "Longer settled groups," writes Nathan Glazer, "have always feared that new immigrant groups might prove disloyal. . . . [In World War I] the fear of disloyalty was so pronounced that German-Americans as a distinct and self-assertive ethnic group more or less went underground. . . . By World War II, few people worried that German-Americans (or Italian-Americans, more recent immigrants) might be disloyal. But Japanese-Americans were made to suffer far more than had the Germans in World War I" (1985, 209). In 1978, James Coleman, as he summarized discussion at a conference on the politics of Spanish and English in the United States, spoke of "the fears of the English native speaking population. One is the fear of cultural and linguistic divisiveness in the society," Coleman said, "and the second is fear of a loss of cultural dominance" (1980, 164). To alleviate such fears, a typical response is a campaign for Americanization, "a consciously articulated movement to strip the immigrant of his native culture and attachments and make him over into an American along Anglo-Saxon lines—all this to be accomplished with great rapidity" (Gordon 1989, 224).

Discussion of Anglo-conformity is too often clouded by the equation of criticism with opposition to literacy and standard languages, with devotion to secession and the replacement of English as the dominant language of the Union. It is sad, yet amusing, to have to say in consequence that secession is unthinkable and standard English irreplaceable in a nation where irresponsible rhetoric would be less tolerable if the blessings of literacy were more widely showered. Believable arguments for or against alternatives to Anglo-conformity should not rest on the imagining of evil but on available knowledge of the world as best we can envision it. For example, since Spanish is often considered the greatest present threat to the dominance of English in the United States, Anglos should be aware of living conditions among Hispanics, the youngest, fastest-growing, and most highly urbanized population in the nation, often confined to "segregated neighborhoods in deteriorating inner cities" (Hispanic Policy Development Project, 1984, vol. 1, 10). For Hispanics, the rates of poverty and unemployment are much higher than for Anglos, and the rate of dropping out from high school among Mexican-American and Puerto Rican students is more than twice the rate for Anglos—understandably, since most Hispanics attend schools where minorities are the majority, schools which are often overcrowded, poorly equipped, and underfunded. Such conditions suggest the possible creation of a permanent underclass in the land of opportunity.

Citation of just one more fact should convince even skeptical suburbanites that there is danger—danger to them—in punitive measures like an English Language Amendment. On April 8, 1989, a former vice chairman of the Democratic National Committee, Polly Baca, told students at the University of Texas that the minority population of the United States will reach 40 percent within their lifetimes and will pass 50 percent in the second half of the twenty-first century. Some time around 2080, Baca said, "we will be a nation where minorities will be the majority" (Tindol 1989, 10). Anglos, it should be obvious, must either accept the end of Anglo-conformity or must prepare themselves to impose an American system of apartheid.

That choice ought to be easy, given the experience of the Deep South and the nation's professed ideals of liberty and equality, brotherhood and sisterhood, opportunity for all. Coercion rouses opposition; justice invites respect. Citizens who are troubled by drug trafficking and uncontrolled immigration might urge a foreign policy which will not make deserts but alleviate suffering in Southeast Asia and Latin America. At home, citizens whose own ancestors were immigrants should respect immigrant languages and cultures, make Americanization attractive, not forbidding, and pay more than lip service to the ideals of the indivisible nation. Indivisibility does not imply uniformity in a country where a Greek from Massachusetts can contest the presidency with an oilman from Maine who pretends to be a Texan while a Black from Chicago makes better sense than either of them. Indivisibility does forbid the present splitting of the population into a shrinking minority of haves and a growing majority of have-nots.

To conclude more lightly: it has been well said of language loyalty that no wife should expect fidelity from a husband who is disrespectful of his mother. In the words of a leading student of English as a world language, Manfred Görlach: "As long as English competence means that the speaker stands a chance of being accepted as equal in American society, the social motivation to master it, and master it with grace and skill, will so predominate that non-English language maintenance is likely, in most communities, to be relegated to the nostalgic niches of folklore, and non-English language maintenance will then be of no greater danger to the American way of life than chow mein, smorgasbord, sauerkraut, paella, or macaroni are to the American menu" (1986, 101).

Notes

1. I have taken the term *Anglo-conformity* from Milton Gordon (1989), who took it from Stewart and Mildred Cole (1954).

Works Cited

Academic Preparation for College. 1983. New York: College Board.

Alatis, James E. 1986. "Comment: The Question of Language Policy." In *International Journal of the Sociology of Language* 60: *The Question of an Official Lan-*

guage: Language Rights and the English Language Amendment, edited by Joshua A. Fishman, 197–200. Amsterdam: Mouton de Gruyter.

Cafferty, Pastora San Juan. 1980. "Bilingualism in America." In *Politics and Language: Spanish and English in the United States,* edited by D.J.R. Bruckner, 1–12. Chicago: University of Chicago Center for Policy Study.

Cole, Stewart G., and Mildred Wiese Cole. 1954. *Minorities and the American Promise.* New York: Harper & Row. (See chapter 6.)

Coleman, James. 1980. "Final Discussion and Summary." In *Politics and Language: Spanish and English in the United States,* edited by D.J.R. Bruckner, 163–67. Chicago: University of Chicago Center for Policy Study.

Conrad, Andrew W., and Joshua A. Fishman. 1977. "English as a World Language: The Evidence." In *The Spread of English,* edited by Andrew W. Conrad, Joshua A. Fishman, and Robert L. Cooper, 3–76. Rowley, Mass.: Newbury House.

Copperman, Paul. 1980. *The Literacy Hoax: The Decline of Reading, Writing, and Learning in the Public Schools and What We Can Do about It.* New York: Morrow.

Epstein, Noel. 1980. "Bilingual Education in the United States: The "either/or" Mistake." In *Politics and Language: Spanish and English in the United States,* edited by D.J.R. Bruckner, 85–110. Chicago: University of Chicago Center for Policy Study.

Fishman, Joshua A. 1981. "Language Policy: Past, Present, and Future." In *Language in the USA,* edited by Charles A. Ferguson and Shirley Brice Heath, 516–26. Cambridge, Mass.: Cambridge University Press.

Glazer, Nathan. 1985. "The Political Distinctiveness of the Mexican-Americans." In *Mexican-Americans in Comparative Perspective,* edited by Walker Connor, 207–24). Washington, D.C.: Urban Institute Press.

Gonzalez, Roseann Dueñas, Alice A. Schott, and Victoria F. Vasquez. 1988. "The English Language Amendment: Examining Myths." *English Journal 77,* no. 3: 24–30.

Gordon, Milton. 1989. "Assimilation in America." In *Rereading America: Cultural Contexts for Critical Thinking and Writing,* edited by Gary Colombo, Robert Cullen, and Bonnie Lisle, 221–29. New York: St. Martin's. (See p. 222, n. 1.)

Görlach, Manfred. 1986. "Comment." In *International Journal of the Sociology of Language 60: The Question of an Official Language: Language Rights and the English Language Amendment,* edited by Joshua A. Fishman, 97–103. Amsterdam: Mouton de Gruyter.

Hakuta, Kenji. 1986. *Mirror of Language: The Debate on Bilingualism.* New York: Basic Books.

Heath, Shirley Brice. 1981. "English in Our Language Heritage." In *Language in the USA,* edited by Charles A. Ferguson and Shirley Brice Heath, 6–20. Cambridge, Mass.: Cambridge University Press.

Heath, Shirley Brice. 1985. "Language Policies: Patterns of Retention and Maintenance." In *Mexican-Americans in Comparative Perspective,* edited by Walker Connor, 259–82. Washington, D.C.: Urban Institute Press.

Hirsch, E. D., Jr. 1987. *Cultural Literacy: What Every American Needs to Know.* Boston: Houghton Mifflin.

Hirsch, E. D., Jr., Joseph F. Kett, and James Trefil. 1988. *The Dictionary of Cultural Literacy*. Boston: Houghton Mifflin.

Hispanic Policy Development Project. 1984. *"Make Something Happen": Hispanics and Urban High School Reform*, 2 vols. Washington, D.C.: Hispanic Policy Development Project.

"Jolly Good! Americans Get a Gold Star in English." 1980. *The New York Times* 50, no. 44, 776 (late city edition, 23 November): 9.

Kachru, Braj B. 1982. "Introduction: The Other Side of English." In *The Other Tongue: English Across Cultures*, 1–12. Urbana: University of Illinois Press.

Lopez, David E. 1982a. *Language Maintenance and Shift in the United States: The Basic Patterns and Their Social Implications*. Los Alamitos, Ca.: National Center for Bilingual Research.

———. 1982b. *"The Maintenance of Spanish over Three Generations in the United States."* Los Alamitos, Ca.: National Center for Bilingual Research.

Marshall, David F. 1986. "The Question of an Official Language: Language Rights and the English Language Amendment." In *International Journal of the Sociology of Language* 60: *The Question of an Official Language: Language Rights and the English Language Amendment*, edited by Joshua A. Fishman, 7–75. Amsterdam: Mouton de Gruyter.

McClellan, Tom. 1989. "Dear Dr. Hayakawa. . . ." *The Texas Observer* 81, no. 4: 17.

National Commission on Excellence in Education. 1983. *A Nation at Risk: The Imperative for Educational Reform*. Washington, D.C.: U.S. Government Printing Office.

Newman, Edwin. 1974. *Strictly Speaking: Will America Be the Death of English?* Indianapolis: Bobbs-Merrill.

Quirk, Randolph, Sidney Greenbaum, Geoffrey Leech, and Jan Svartvik. 1985. *A Comprehensive Grammar of the English Language*. London: Longman.

Simon, John. 1980. "Edwin Newman Bares His Civil Tongue." In *Paradigms Lost: Reflections on Literacy and Its Decline*, 58–61. New York: Clarkson N. Potter.

Tindol, Robert. 1989. "An Ethnically Diverse World." *On Campus* (the University of Texas at Austin), 17–23 April, 10.

Wardhaugh, Ronald. 1987. *Languages in Competition: Dominance, Diversity, and Decline*. Oxford and London: Blackwell and Deutsch.

IV Responding to the English-Only Movement

10 Disillusionment with Official English and the Search for Alternatives

Mary Carol Combs
University of Arizona

Lynn M. Lynch

The movement in the United States to declare English the official language has gradually gained momentum since Congress first held hearings on a proposed English Language Amendment to the Constitution in 1984. In the past six years, legislators in at least 30 different states have considered official-English bills. In addition, voters in several states—including California in 1986 and Arizona, Colorado, and Florida in 1988—have approved official language legislation, bringing the total number of "official-English" states as of mid-1989 to 16. Some observers speculate that this number may increase, given the strong support for official-English measures indicated in recent public opinion polls (Crawford 1988b, 2).

Despite widespread support for official English, however, there is growing evidence that the movement has lost some of its appeal, even among its most influential supporters. For instance, revelations in 1988 about a "hidden agenda" with racist overtones have caused many advocates to reexamine the motivation behind restrictive language measures. Furthermore, the damaging effects of recently enacted official-English legislation are now well documented and indisputable: minority language speakers are encountering hostility and discrimination as a direct result of the new language laws on the books. In light of these developments, other, more positive language policies that stress the benefits of multilingualism are attracting support and gaining credibility as viable alternatives to official-English in the United States.

Disillusionment within the Ranks

One of the most common arguments used for official English is that language legislation is needed to force immigrants to learn English.

99

Studies indicate, however, that non-native English speakers are assimilating into the English-speaking culture of the United States at least as rapidly as they did a century ago, if not more so (Veltman 1988, 3, 22–29, 46–50). The problem is not that immigrants won't learn English; on the contrary, there are simply not enough English classes and teachers to fill the current demand.

Ironically, when Proposition 63—the California constitutional amendment establishing English as the official state language—was passed in November 1986, more than 40,000 people were on waiting lists for English instruction in Los Angeles alone (Woo 1986, 1). During that contentious campaign, author Norman Cousins expressed his concern over this discrepancy by resigning from the advisory board of U.S. English, the leading national organization promoting English as the official language. Said Cousins, "Not until we provide educational facilities for all who are now standing in line waiting to take lessons in English should we presume to pass judgment on the non-English-speaking people in our midst." Cousins also noted the "very real danger" of racial discrimination that passage of the proposition would bring (Twombley 1986, 3).

Another argument for official language legislation is that the primacy of English is imperiled in the United States. As proof of this "threat to our common linguistic bond," official-English supporters point to the continuing influx of certain groups of immigrants, such as Hispanics and Asians, many of whom choose to remain actively bilingual. Yet linguistic studies show that the children of immigrants are less apt than their parents to use their native language; by the second generation, the majority speak only English. Furthermore, it is clear that as long as English remains the high-status language in the United States—and there is every reason to believe that it will—there is no danger of its being displaced by other languages, no matter how high the rate of native language retention among immigrants. In fact, minority languages are threatened by English, not the other way around (Veltman 1988, 3, 22–29, 46–50).

The real issue is not language policy—a respectable topic for discussion; rather, it is the growing minority population in the United States. Although many official-English supporters are genuinely—albeit mistakenly—concerned about the status of English in the United States, there is incontrovertible evidence that the agenda of the movement's most powerful organization, U.S. English, stems from racist sentiments.

In October 1988, *The Arizona Republic* published portions of an internal memorandum written in 1986 by John Tanton, one of the founders of U.S. English. Intended for a private discussion group, it expresses concerns about the twenty-first century, when minority groups—particularly Latin Americans—will likely have greater influence in both the business and political sectors. Among the questions Tanton poses concerning the "consequences of immigration" are the following:

> As Whites see their power and control over their lives declining, will they simply go quietly into the night? Or will there be an explosion? Why don't non-Hispanic Whites have a group identity, as do Blacks, Jews, Hispanics?
>
> Is apartheid in Southern California's future? . . . The non-Hispanic Whites and Asians will own the property, have the good jobs and education, speak one language and be mostly Protestant and "other." The Blacks and Hispanics will have the poor jobs, will lack education, own little property, speak another language and will be mainly Catholic. . . . Will this prove a social and political San Andreas Fault?

Tanton points specifically to the dangers of a high birth rate among immigrants:

> "To govern is to populate." . . . Will the present majority peaceably hand over its political power to a group that is simply more fertile?
>
> Can *homo contraceptivus* compete with *homo progenitiva* if borders aren't controlled? Or is advice to limit ones [sic] family simple advice to move over and let someone else with greater reproductive powers occupy the space? . . . Perhaps this is the first instance in which those with their pants up are going to get caught by those with their pants down!

In addition to "greater reproductive powers," Tanton cites what he views as other undesirable characteristics of immigrants, notably Hispanics: a high educational dropout rate, the *mordida* (bribing public officials), the "lack of involvement in public affairs," and Catholicism (which Tanton suggests has implications for the separation of church and state), to name just a few (Tanton 1986). The language issue is mentioned only in passing.

The publication of the Tanton memo caused much embarrassment and led to several resignations, including that of veteran newsman Walter Cronkite, who quit the U.S. English advisory board. Said Cronkite, "I . . . cannot favor legislation that could even remotely be interpreted to restrict the civil rights or the educational opportunities of our minority population" ("Walter Cronkite," 1988, B1). U.S. English President Linda Chavez, an influential politician who, like Cronkite, had lent credibility to the movement, also condemned the memo. Calling it "repugnant," she demanded—and later received—Tanton's resignation from the Board of Directors (Von Drehle 1988, A1). Chavez herself subsequently resigned following additional revelations about contributions to Tanton's organizational network ("Official-English," 1988). According to investigators, from 1981 to 1986 the Tanton-founded Federation of American Immigration Reform (FAIR) received $370,000 from the Pioneer Fund, a little-known foundation that promotes "racial betterment" through eugenics (Crawford 1988a).

Official-English Fallout

The legal ramifications of official-English legislation are still unclear. Many statutes, for example, simply declare English the official language, just as a bill might symbolically recognize, say, a state flower or bird. Nevertheless, passage of any official language legislation has potentially damaging consequences.

The proscriptive version of the English Language Amendment (ELA), for example, strictly prohibits the use of languages other than English by federal, state, and local governments. Thus, bilingual programs and interpreter services currently available in the areas of education, voting, the legal system, social services, and health care—all services which have been criticized by ELA supporters at one time or another—would be in jeopardy.

The "revised" version of the ELA, introduced in early 1989, would also jeopardize many programs designed to aid immigrants' integration into mainstream society. Although the bill exempts laws that protect public health and safety, allow for courtroom translators, and provide for educational opportunities for limited-English-proficient speakers, it fails to preserve a broad range of multilingual services. These include bilingual voting assistance, job training and referral services, welfare and Social Security notices, and other programs that do not come under the category of "protecting public health and safety."

On the state level, official-English legislation ranges from one nonbinding resolution (Georgia) and various statutes to a handful of constitutional amendments, which tend to have stronger language and thus more tangible or far-reaching effects than do statutes. The Arizona amendment, for example, is the most restrictive state language legislation to date. In addition to establishing English as the official language of the state, it requires all sectors of the state government to "act in English and in no other language." Further, no government document, law, order, decree, or policy is deemed valid or effective unless it is in English. Since the new law became effective in 1988, the legality of several kinds of services has been called into question. These services include bilingual lottery tickets and the use of non-English languages by state lottery officials; Motor Vehicle Division pamphlets and oral explanations of licensing procedures in languages other than English; promotional brochures published in Japanese, German, and French by the state Office of Tourism; and the designation of highways, streets, bridges, or towns in languages other than English (Corbin 1989).

California's language amendment, which became effective in 1986, is also fairly restrictive. For instance, it bars the state legislature from passing any law that "diminishes or ignores the role of English as the common language." In addition, it gives residents the right to sue to have the amendment enforced, thus making the use of any language other than English in public or business settings a possible violation of the law. Indeed, since Proposition 63 was passed, the number of "English-only" rules in the workplace has increased. There has also been a marked increase in the number of municipal ordinances regulating commercial use of bilingual signs: in some town English letters must now be at least one-third to one-half higher than the letters or characters of other languages on the sign.

While the legal effects of official English are disputable, the social consequences are not. Since passage of language amendments and statutes in various states, minority language speakers have encountered hostility and distrust to a greater degree than before. For example, several incidents involving harassment or discrimination have been reported in Florida since a language amendment was approved there in 1988:

- A supermarket cashier in Coral Gables was suspended without pay for speaking Spanish on the job (Garcia 1988, D1).
- A monthly mortgage check was returned to a Miami resident because it was written in Spanish (May 1988, B1).
- Telephone operators have reportedly refused to take calls in Spanish, insisting that such calls can only be accepted now in English (Ingwerson 1988, 3).
- Immediately following the election, one Spanish-language radio station reported receiving up to 30 calls a day from people complaining they had been harassed, insulted, shunned, or hurt simply for speaking Spanish (May 1988, B1).

Although at least some of the actions described above are illegal (in the first instance, the worker was reinstated to his job and the manager transferred to another store), they illustrate the socially divisive climate engendered by official-English legislation. In addition, they show the damage caused by individuals attempting to enforce laws they do not understand.

Complaints about discrimination and harassment have also been reported in Colorado, which, like Florida, passed a language amendment in 1988. For example,

- A bus driver in Mesa County allegedly told Hispanic children they could no longer speak Spanish on the bus (Williams 1988, 8).

- A fast food restaurant manager prevented an employee from translating the menu for a South American patron (Gavin 1988, A1).

- An opposition group, Coloradans for Language Freedom, has reported receiving racist phone calls at its office (Gavin 1988, A1).

Again, such cases point to the danger of passing legislation that encourages hostility toward minority language speakers and leads to citizens' arbitrary enforcement of the law.

English Plus

In response to the current trend toward language restrictionism in the United States and the growing negative publicity surrounding the official-English movement, opponents have begun uniting to offer a positive alternative: "English Plus." Unlike official English (also known, appropriately, as English-only), English Plus promotes the idea of English *plus* other languages. For the limited-English speaker, this means expanded opportunities to acquire English-language proficiency skills—*plus* mastery of other subjects—through instruction in one's native language, if necessary. For the native English speaker, English Plus means English *plus* mastery of a second or multiple languages.

In both cases, individuals are encouraged to retain or improve their native language skills while learning other subjects, including non-native languages. Thus, English Plus promotes bilingualism among native English speakers and non-native English speakers alike. More importantly, it guarantees that all individuals in the United States are afforded equal educational opportunities regardless of their linguistic background.

The English Plus concept was first conceived in response to a speech in September 1985 given by former Secretary of Education

William Bennett. Bennett declared that the educational sector in the United States had "lost sight of the goal of learning English as the key to equal educational opportunity" (Bennett 1985). A Miami-based civil rights and educational group called the Spanish-American League Against Discrimination (SALAD) responded to Bennett's claims by issuing a document which was to become the blueprint for the English Plus concept: "We fear that Secretary Bennett has lost sight of the fact that English is *a* key to equal opportunity. . . . English by itself is not enough." The SALAD document declared, "Not English ONLY—English *PLUS!*" (SALAD 1985, 4). Before long, SALAD and LULAC began to use the term "English Plus" to represent the new movement in support of bilingual education and alternatives to English-only.

In 1987—just two years after "English Plus" was coined—the English Plus Information Clearinghouse (EPIC) was established as a joint project of the National Immigration, Refugee, and Citizenship Forum and the Joint National Committee for Languages. A national clearinghouse based in Washington, D.C., EPIC was created to provide opportunities for informed public debate on language policy and language rights in the United States, as well as to promote positive, alternative policies to the official-English movement. Accordingly, EPIC's founders declared the need to "defeat any legislative initiative on the federal, state, or local level which would mandate English as the official language" and to work toward "a vastly expanded network of facilities and programs for comprehensive instruction in English and other languages" (EPIC 1987).

Since Epic's founding, many diverse groups have expressed their support for English Plus alternatives, including the American Civil Liberties Union, the American Jewish Committee, the Center for Applied Linguistics, the Mexican-American Legal Defense and Educational Fund, the National Council of Teachers of English, and Teachers of English to Speakers of Other Languages. At the same time, Atlanta, Cleveland, Dallas, Tucson, and Washington, D.C., among other municipalities, have passed "multicultural resolutions" that officially recognize the linguistic and cultural diversity of their respective communities. A number of states, including Connecticut, New Mexico, Oregon, Pennsylvania, and Washington, have considered or have already passed similar resolutions.

Several groups have organized in individual states to combat the negative effects of official-English legislation and to advocate minority language rights. One such group is the National Coalition for Language Freedom, a predominantly West Coast-based membership organization devoted entirely to opposing the official-English movement and related legislation. In addition to organizing letter-writing campaigns to Congress to oppose the English Language Amendment, the coalition works toward educating local communities about the dangers of language restrictionism.

On the national level, two language-related measures have been introduced in Congress as a result of efforts by coalitions to promote alternative language policies. One bill, the English Proficiency Act (later renamed the English Literacy Grant Program), was brought before Congress at the request of a coalition of national Hispanic organizations concerned about the paucity of literacy classes available for limited-English-proficient individuals in the United States. Signed into law in 1988 and still awaiting funding, the bill provides grants to states for the establishment, operation, and improvement of English literacy programs for limited-English-proficient adults and out-of-school youth. Another bill, the Cultural Rights Amendment, was introduced as a direct alternative to the English Language Amendment. Conceived by the Federation of American Cultural and Language Communities, it recognizes the "right of people to preserve, foster, and promote their respective historic, linguistic, and cultural origins." The official-English movement has managed, over the course of just a few years, to bring the issue of language rights in the United States to the fore—a positive step, were it not for the restrictive stance it has adopted and the socially divisive climate it has fostered. Instead of a precious national resource to be protected, linguistic diversity in the United States is increasingly viewed as a threat not only to English but to the social fabric of the country as well. Yet the "threat" is not languages other than English but the people who speak them. The legal protection of English merely serves as a smoke screen for a fundamentally racist movement directed against certain minority groups, particularly Hispanics.

Ironically, it is English *Plus*, not English-*only*, that holds the greatest promise for a unified society in which no one group—majority or minority—feels threatened. In fact, encouraging all citizens to become proficient in more than one language, as well as preserving the many diverse languages spoken in the nation, is the only rational policy in a multi-ethnic, yet increasingly interdependent world. As English Plus advocates recognize, linguistic and ethnic differences are a *positive* force, and one that is becoming more important as we approach the twenty-first century. Indeed, no one group will, as Tanton wonders, "simply go quietly into the night"—and for that Americans can be thankful.

Works Cited

Bennett, Willlam. 1985. Speech to Association for a Better New York. New York City. 26 September.

Corbin, Robert. [Arizona Attorney General.] 1989. Opinion on the Constitutionality of Proposition 106. 24 January.

Crawford, James. 1988a. "Official English Attracting Bizarre Followers." *Mesa Tribune*. 22 October.

———. 1988b. "The Language Policy Debate: Implications for Educational Equity." Unpublished Speech at the Mid Atlantic Equity Center, American University, Bethesda, Md. 18 February.

English Plus Information Clearinghouse (EPIC). 1987. Statement of Purpose. 20 October.

Garcia, Luciano. 1988. "Publix Disciplines Worker for Speaking Spanish on the Job." *The Miami Herald*, 12 November, D1.

Gavin, Jennifer. 1988. "Pena Outlaws Bias Based on Language." *Denver Post* 97, no. 149 (28 December): Al.

Ingwerson, Marshall. 1988. "English-Only Laws: How Broad?" *The Christian Science Monitor* 81, no. 3 (29 November): B1.

May, Patrick. 1988. "On-the-Job Conflicts Erupt over Spanish." *The Miami Herald*, 20 November, B1.

"Official-English Leader Quits." 1988. *Rocky Mountain News*, 18 October.

Spanish-American League Against Discrimination (SALAD) Education Committee. 1985. "Not English Only, English *Plus!*" Unpublished manuscript. 15 October, 4.

Tanton, John. 1986. Memorandum to WITAN IV Attendees. 10 October, 1–2.

Twombley, William. 1986. "Norman Cousins Drops His Support of Proposition 63." *Los Angeles Times*, 16 October, 3.

Veltman, Calvin. 1988. *The Future of the Spanish Language in the United States.* Washington, D.C.: Hispanic Policy Development Project.

Von Drehle, Dave. 1988. "English-Only Leader Urged to Quit." *The Miami Herald*, 15 October, A1.

"Walter Cronkite Quits Board of U.S. English." 1988. *Tempe Tribune*, 14 October, B1.

Williams, Leroy, Jr. 1988. "Pena Signs Order Protecting Non-English Speakers." *Rocky Mountain News*, 28 December, 8.

Woo, Ellen. 1986. "Immigrants—A Rush to the Classrooms." *Los Angeles Times*, 16 October, 1.

11 The "Mis-education of the Negro"—and You Too

Geneva Smitherman
Michigan State University

In 1933, Dr. Carter G. Woodson, the African-American, Harvard-trained historian, published his analysis of the education of Black people. Entitled *Mis-education of the Negro*, Woodson's analysis was based on forty years of experience in the education of "black, brown, yellow and white races in both hemispheres and in tropical and temperate regions . . . in all grades from the kindergarten to the university" (xxix). The central thesis of this scholar-activist—whose 1926 inauguration of Negro History Week laid the foundation for today's Black History Month—is that the educational curriculum does not reflect the true history, sociology, politics, economics—nor language—of Americans:

> The description of the various parts of the world was worked out according to the same plan. The parts inhabited by the Caucasian were treated in detail. Less attention was given to the yellow people, still less to the red, very little to the brown, and practically none to the black race. (18)

This "drifting from the truth" in the education of African-Americans since emancipation had, by 1933, resulted in the "mis-education of the Negro." But beyond that, the "educational system . . . is an antiquated process which does not hit the mark even in the case of the needs of the white man himself . . ." (xxxii). The educational deprivation of *all* Americans begins in youth and crystallizes in an adult society characterized by "deep-seated insecurities, intra-racial cleavages, and inter-racial antagonisms" (viii). Mis-educated adults are served up more mis-education in college, they return to the public schools to train and mis-educate youth, and this mind-set is perpetrated for generations.

The year was 1933, but Woodson's message has an all-too-familiar ring over half a century later. The English-only movement represents a specific instance of the continuing mis-education of the people of the United States. This article will propose a National Language Policy and concomitant political strategies for intervention in this vicious cycle in order to bring to a halt the "mis-education of the Negro"—and you too.

From Jumpstreet

Wie geht's? Qué tal? What up doe? The true history of America is one that reflects large numbers of citizens who have continued to speak "English plus" since the pre-Revolutionary War era. This has been the case even for African-Americans. In spite of all attempts to strip the enslaved African population of its language and culture, it is clear that the first slaves, who, in 1619, were brought to what would become the United States, spoke pidgin English as well as their own West African tongues. In subsequent years, the pidgin English became an English creole, existing alongside the White English spoken by some Africans in the slave community. Similarly, Native Americans, who were here before Columbus and before the *Mayflower*, continued to maintain their own languages even as some of them learned the English of the white settlers who would decimate their ranks in years to come. During the Revolutionary War, proclamations of the Continental Congress were printed in German and French (Kloss 1977, 26). In subsequent years, several state constitutions were printed in languages other than English. For instance, Colorado's constitution, which was adopted over a hundred years ago, was printed in English, Spanish, and French (Landers 1989, 26). During World War I, the federal government advertised its liberty bonds in every language used in the United States (Kloss 1977, 33). As we approach the dawning of the twenty-first century, 32 million Americans (or 19.7 percent of the population) report that a mother tongue other than English was spoken in their childhood homes, and 18 million indicate that they currently speak a language other than English at home (Bureau of the Census 1979, 5). By no means are these speakers all located in California, New York City, or the Southwest, nor is Spanish the only foreign language. In my home state, Michigan, for instance, there are at least 90,178 speakers of Polish (Bureau of the Census 1980, 292, table 236).[1]

Not only is the United States diverse in terms of the many non-English-language groups, there may be as many as the proverbial fifty-seven varieties of American English, depending on how you slice the pie. In New York City, there is a moving company known as "Schleppers," taking its name after the popular New York verb *schlep*, to carry or move (Alvarez and Kolker 1987). In Jackson, Mississippi, you *take sick*, but in Chicago, Illinois, you *get sick*. And the response to the Black English greeting "What up doe?" in standard English is "I'm fine. How are you?"

The United States *is* a land of many voices; it *is* a nation of many cultures. Its diversity has been its strength. Despite one or two shameful moments when there were attempts to suppress this diversity— e.g., the incarceration of Japanese-American citizens during World War II—the appeal, the pull of the United States has been its embrace and celebration of cultural and linguistic diversity. (You know, the Statue of Liberty, out there in New York Harbor, bees saying, "All y'all come now.") The success of the American democratic experiment is manifest in the many tongues and many cultures of the United States, in the hyphenated citizens, who have proudly retained their native heritage while simultaneously adopting U.S. culture. Most citizens will quickly and with pride tell you that they are Italian-American, German-American, Polish-American, etc.[2] The reality, then, is that there is a living heritage of linguistic-cultural diversity in the United States. Kloss eloquently sums up the true linguistic history of the United States:

> One notion dear to Americans has been that the American society has wrought miracles in assimilating the numberless hordes of non-English immigrants. . . . The popular image of the United States as a nation united by one language and one culture has always been illusory. . . . Although the American melting pot has indeed fused millions of second-and-third generation immigrant families into unilingual English-speaking Americans, unmelted or partially melted millions have also survived . . . [and maintained] their ethnic identity in their new and spacious land. . . . It is only fitting that it should be so. For the concepts of diversity and political pluralism are the very ones which permitted the creation of the United States. (1977, vii–xiii)

Back-slidin'

English is the native language of twelve nations and an official or semiofficial language in thirty-three more nations. It is the first language of 345 million people and the second language of another 400 million (MacKaye 1988, 23). As anyone who has traveled abroad knows, English speakers can expect to be understood in most major cities of the world. Fishman et al. (1977) have called this the "century of English."

At the same time that English has spread, however, the perception and image of the United States have deteriorated around the world. Because of its often reactionary policies in the Mideast and in Central and Latin America, its reluctance to withdraw its support from South Africa, its invasion of the tiny little island of Grenada, and similar abuses of its superpower status, the United States is viewed as exploitative, imperialistic, and supportive of oppressive governments. Further, as the Third World has insisted on its share of the international economic pie—and I count Japan among this group—the U.S. economy has suffered. The response of U.S. multinational corporations has been to tighten the reins here at home by closing plants, relocating industries to nonunionized states, and extracting wage concessions from workers.

In the last decade, the highest proportion of births in the United States has been to people of color, and the vast majority of immigrants to the United States are brown, yellow, and black people from Third World countries. In 1985, 89 percent of the *legal* immigrants, that is, 653,639 persons, came from non-white areas of the world—Asia, Central America, South America, Mexico, Africa, the West Indies, the Pacific Islands (MacKaye 1988, 60). However, despite the continued influx of monolingual immigrants, which would appear to delay the learning of English, research shows that, for example, many Hispanics are not only bilingual, but go on to become English monolinguals by the second generation and most by the third generation (Veltman 1988, 47). And surveys by linguists and researchers indicate that 96–98 percent of Americans speak English well or very well (Zentella 1988; Califa 1989).

In this historical moment, S. I. Hayakawa introduced the English Language Amendment bill (ELA). The year was 1981, during Hayakawa's reign as senator. The bill called for an amendment to the U.S. Constitution to make English the official language of the United States. In 1983, Hayakawa and Dr. John Tanton founded U.S. English, a lobbying group for the ELA. And in November 1988, Colorado, the same state that had printed its constitution in three languages a little over a hundred years ago, passed an amendment to its state constitution making English the official language of that state.

In addition to his work with U.S. English, Tanton is founder of the Federation for American Immigration Reform (whose acronym, ironically, is FAIR). This organization is devoted to curbing immigration into the United States, although there has been no outcry against European immigration, only that of people of color. Tanton, an ophthalmologist residing in Petoskey, Michigan—if me and him coexisting in the same state ain living proof of democratic pluralism, I don't know what is!—wrote a memo to a group called "WITAN" (Old English for "wise men"), which surfaced in the fall of 1988 (Crawford 1989, 57). That memo makes racially offensive remarks about Hispanics:

> Will the present majority peaceably hand over its poitical power to a group that is simply more fertile? Is apartheid in Southern Cali-

fornia's future? As whites see their power and control over their
lives declining, will they simply go quietly into the night? Or will
there be an explosion? ... Perhaps this is the first instance in which
those with their pants up are going to get caught by those with
their pants down. (Hacker 1989, 3A, 6A).

In a Detroit bar a few years ago, a Chinese man, Vincent Chen, was
beaten to death by two white men, one of whom had recently been laid
off from his job in a Detroit automobile plant. Thinking Chen was
Japanese, he yelled out, "There's one of those [expletive] who's taking
all our jobs." The two of them then beat Chen to death but were
acquitted of murder charges.

Be What You Is Instead of What You Ain,
Cause If You Ain What You Is,
Then You Isn't What You Ain

It is clear that the United States is troubled and seeking quick-fix
solutions to its staggering and complex problems. The movement to
suppress linguistic-cultural diversity passes itself off as a unity movement and cloaks itself in red-white-blue apple pie. We are told that a
common language is the tie that binds. But U.S. history belies that.
Although the nation has been linguistically and culturally diverse
from Jumpstreet, the common thread of unity has been our shared
values around and belief in the democratic ideal, that all men—and
women, at least since 1920!—are created equal, and that all people,
regardless of race, color, creed, sex, or national origin, have the right to
life, liberty, and the pursuit of happiness.

To be sure, inequality still exists, for women, people of color, the
white unworking class, and others. Yes, for a lot of folk, the American
Dream turned into a nightmare. And yes, as African-American poet
Haki Madhubuti says, the pot melted and we burned. But the recognition of this lingering inequality is what the movements of the 1960s
and 1970s made this nation face up to. Spearheaded by the black
liberation movement, other groups, who, like African-Americans, had
been "invisible," began to assert their claim to equality—Native Americans, women, Hispanics, Asian-Americans, the disabled, senior citizens, gays, and others who had not shared equally in the pursuit of the
American Dream. It was that motion of history that produced teacher
education programs in linguistic and cultural diversity, the "Students'
Right to Their Own Language," the eradication of speech tests for
teacher certification, and the King ("Black English") case.

In 1972, the "Students' Right to Their Own Language" became the policy of the Conference on College Composition and Communication (Butler 1974). It was conceived to promote language rights for *all* students, not just black or brown. Its objective was to establish the right of students to have their home language respected and accepted in the educational environment, even as the students acquired the language of wider communication, so-called standard English. It was a policy in recognition of the linguistic-cultural diversity inherent in the United States being what it is instead of what it ain.

The 1979 King decision established that the Ann Arbor, Michigan School District had been guilty of not providing educational equity to the Black English-speaking children attending the Martin Luther King, Jr., Elementary School (see, e.g., Smitherman 1981). Instead of taking the children's language into account in teaching them, the school had simply classified them as learning disabled, placed them in speech therapy, and segregated them off into special classes where they were going nowhere. Federal Judge Charles C. Joiner's opinion acknowledged that Black English was a legitimate language, that lack of familiarity with Black English, as with "German," could produce a "language barrier," and that the school had to "take it into account" in teaching students to "read in the standard English of the school, the commercial world, the arts, science, and professions" (Joiner 1981 [1979], 338; see also Joiner 1978).

As chief consultant and expert witness for the parents and their children in the King case, I was painfully reminded of my experience in a college speech therapy class many years before. Because of my Black English, I had failed the standard speech articulation test required in those days in over forty states for teacher certification. This regressive policy was eradicated in the era of enlightened social struggle of the previous generation that embraced the linguistic-cultural diversity that is the essence of the American Experience. As the daughter of a sharecropper, who at the time I completed seventh grade, became the first in my lineage to do so, and as a result of the activist struggles of my people, went on to a major university and earned a Ph.D., I here bear witness to the reality that out of social struggle, there has been progress. Yeah, we done come a long way, baby, but we still ain come far enough.

Lessons of the Blood

In 1984, in the keynote presentation at the Howard University Black Communications Conference in Washington, D.C., I called for the adoption of a language policy for the African-American community. I proposed a tripartite policy, a "perfect, inseparable trinity": (1) acquisition of the language of wider (note, *wider*, not *whiter!*) communication, so-called standard English (however, "wider communication" more properly speaks to a language that goes beyond one's own community); (2) reinforcement of the legitimacy and maintenance of Black English and implementation of it as a language of coequal instruction; and (3) promotion of one or more Third World languages (Smitherman 1984). In 1986, as a featured speaker at the CCCC Convention, I presented my Black Language Policy again (Smitherman 1986). In the audience was a feminist scholar, Professor Elizabeth Auleta, who challenged me not to limit something that sounded "good for white folk, too." (Of course, how could I have missed it; what is good for African-Americans is usually good for the nation!)

In 1988, the Conference on College Composition and Communication unanimously adopted the National Language Policy developed by its newly appointed Language Policy Committee. Established in 1987, with myself as chair, this committee was charged with developing an organizational response and strategies for the CCCC to counter and combat the English-only movement. The members of the Language Policy Committee are Elizabeth Auleta, Thomas Kochman, Elizabeth McPherson, Guadalupe Valdes, Jeffrey Youdelman, and Ana Celia Zentella. They took my more narrowly conceived Black Language Policy to the next evolutionary stage: a broadened, fully worked-out language policy for the entire nation (Language Policy Committee 1987). The Language Policy Committee's work thus reaffirms the value of collective work and vision.

The CCCC National Language Policy is reproduced in its entirety in the following extract. This policy should be implemented beginning in elementary school, or even preschool, and should continue throughout the educational system. The ultimate objective is to prepare *all* American youth for full participation in our multicultural nation and linguistically diverse world.

BACKGROUND:

There is a need for a National Language Policy, the purpose of which is to prepare everyone in the United States for full participation in a multi-cultural nation. Such a policy recognizes and reflects the historical reality that, even though English has become the language of wider communication, we are a multi-lingual society. All people in a democratic society have the right to equal protection of the laws, to employment, to social services, and to participation in the democratic process. No one should be denied these or any other civil rights because of linguistic and cultural

differences. Legal protection, education, and social services must
be provided in English as well as other languages in order to
enable everyone in the United States to take full advantage of
these rights. This language policy affirms that civil rights should
not be denied to people because of linguistic differences. It enables
everyone to participate in the life of the nation by ensuring continued respect both for English, the common language, and for the
many other languages that have contributed to our rich cultural
and linguistic heritage.

Therefore, be it resolved that CCCC members promote the National Language Policy adopted at the Executive Committee meeting on March 16, 1988. This policy has three inseparable parts:

1. to provide resources to enable native and non-native speakers
   to achieve oral and literate competence in English, the language of wider communication;

2. to support programs that assert the legitimacy of native languages and dialects and ensure that proficiency in the mother
   tongue will not be lost; and

3. to foster the teaching of languages other than English so that
   native speakers of English can rediscover the language of their
   heritage or learn a second language.

Passed unanimously by both the Executive Committee and the
membership at the CCCC Annual Meeting in March, 1988. The
National Language Policy is now the official policy of the CCCC.

For fundamental change to take place that will put a stop once and
for all to the "miseducation of the Negro"—and you too—it is necessary to venture into the political mine fields. The following strategies
have been (or should be) undertaken by educators:

1. Work with elected public officials to propose legislation declaring
   and providing resources to promote a policy of multilingualism.
   This course of action has been undertaken by local English Plus
   coalitions with a victory in one state and a (hopefully) pending
   victory in another. In March 1989, New Mexico's legislature
   passed House Joint Memorial 16 in which it "reaffirms its advo-
   cacy of the teaching of other languages in the United States and
   its belief that the position of English is not threatened." The
   resolution declares that "proficiency . . . in more than one language is to the economic and cultural benefit of our state and the
   nation, whether that proficiency derives from second language
   study by English speakers or from home language maintenance
   plus English acquisition by speakers of other languages" (State of
   New Mexico Thirty-Ninth Legislature 1989). The resolution was
   sent to the governor, the superintendent of instruction, members

of New Mexico's State Board of Education, and the regents of the University of New Mexico. In the state of Michigan in 1985, a law was passed allowing high school credit in a foreign language to students who had attained proficiency in that language *outside* of school (State of Michigan 83rd Legislature 1985). And recently, both houses of the Michigan legislature introduced a proposal in the form of a resolution to "maintain Michigan as a multi-language state." (For details on House Resolution No. 376 and Senate Resolution No. 310, see State of Michigan 1987). The Michigan proposal, which is very similar to New Mexico's, is now in committee.

As another important victory for language education advocates, the National Governors' Association Task Force on International Education recommended not only that foreign language study begin in the first grade and continue throughout schooling, but that foreign languages be taught during the summer, after school, and on weekends. Further, the Task Force recommended that school districts provide inservice teacher training in foreign language and international study (Advocates for Language Learning 1989, 1).

2. Organize campaigns for voters to voice their opposition to pending English Language Amendment legislation on the congressional level. In 1988, during the congressional hearings on ELA, an extensive letter-writing campaign was promoted among churchgoers, community organizations, and other "everyday people." CCCC's Language Policy Committee, the English Plus Information Clearinghouse (EPIC), Michigan's English Plus Coalition, the American Civil Liberties Union, Californians United, and numerous other groups were involved in this concerted effort. At this stage, of course, we are unable to predict the outcome of the ELA. However, the impact of the letter-writing campaign is evident in reactions from congresspersons, such as Congressman John Conyers, in a letter to the CCCC Language Policy Committee, indicating his view that "restrictive 'English-only' legislation has had such bad effects as discouraging performance in schools, making entire communities feel segregated, and discouraging American students from the need to learn foreign languages" (Conyers, personal communication, 1988).

3. Professional organizations must widely publicize their opposition to English-only policies and their support of multilanguage policies and practices. While it is necessary to pass resolutions and work throughout the profession, this action alone is insuffi-

cient. The public and policymakers must be informed of organizational positions and efforts. For example, the leadership of the Conference on College Composition and Communication has written several letters in this vein, both to state and national elected officials—and they virtually always respond (e.g., Schwartz, personal communication, 1988). Current CCCC efforts are in place to target the presidents of state boards of education throughout the country for letters and other forms of communication about this critical issue.

4. Promote progressive thinking about language issues through the media, both print and broadcast (e.g., letters to the editors, opinion editorials, appearance on radio and television news and talk shows). A recent example from the Language Policy Committee was Professor Zentella's February 1989 appearance on a television talk show discussing the narrowness and inadequacy of New York Mayor Koch's list of twenty "speech demons" (e.g., *axe* for *ask*) which has been proposed as the language program for New York City's students (Lewis 1989).

The critical point in all of this is that the public, elected officials, and policymakers greatly benefit from and indeed welcome the expertise and experience of professionals. We cannot afford to be silent, for our efforts can and do bear fruit. English educators, language and composition professionals, must continue to speak the truth to the people about what America *is*: a land of linguistic and cultural diversity. While this might not be what some folk *want* it to be, that's what it is. The United States has welded together diverse peoples and races, with their many tongues and cultures—including even the 35 million African descendants of an enslaved population, including even the millions of descendants of Native American and Spanish intermixture—it has welded together a host of variegated peoples into one nation. This is the essence of America, and it stands as a singular achievement in the history of humankind. A multilanguage policy, such as the CCCC's National Language Policy, and the implementation of multilingual instructional programs throughout America's educational system are a significant beginning in the move to halt mis-education because it speaks to what we *is* instead of what we *ain*.

Auf wiedersehen, Adios, Uhm outa here.

Notes

1. Because the census question did not ask about language spoken in the church or community, but only inquired about language spoken in the home,

local demographers give significantly higher estimates of Polish speakers. For a penetrating critique of census methods that have undoubtedly produced significant undercounts of foreign language speakers, see Hart-Gonzalez and Feingold 1990.

2. I note in passing that Jesse Jackson's call for "Black" to be replaced by "African-American" is right on time and what many African-American intellectuals have long advocated. It symbolizes our connection with Mother Africa while simultaneously affirming, as Langston Hughes once put it, that "we too sing America." Although "Black" was suitable and even necessary in its day, it remains an anomaly that is asymmetrical with the naming practices of America's other groups.

Works Cited

Advocates for Language Learning. 1989. "Governors Stress Foreign Language Education." *Newsletter* 5, no. 1: 1.

Alvarez, L., and A. Kolker. 1987. *American Tongues*. Instructional videotape. New York: Center for New American Media.

Bureau of the Census. 1979. *Current Population Reports,* no. 116 (November). Washington, D.C.: Government Printing Office.

―――. 1980. "Nativity and Language for Divisions and States." In *General Social and Economic Characteristics: United States Summary,* table 236. Washington, D.C.: Government Printing Office.

Butler, M., ed. 1974. "Students' Right to Their Own Language." Special Issue of *College Composition and Communication,* 25(Fall): 1–32.

Califa, A. J. 1989. "English-Only Laws Would Mean Loss of Rights." *Civil Liberties* (Winter).

Conyers, John. [Congressman.] 1988. Personal communication. 15 August.

Crawford, J. 1989. *Bilingual Education: History, Politics, Theory, and Practice.* Trenton: Crane Publishing.

Fishman, J., R. Cooper, and A. Conrad. 1977. *The Spread of English.* Rowley: Newbury House.

Hacker, D. 1989. "Petoskey Doctor Leads English-Only Crusade." *Detroit Free Press,* 14 February, 3A.

Hart-Gonzalez, L., and M. Feingold. 1990. "Retention of Spanish in the Home." *International Journal of Sociolinguistics,* no. 83 (Special Issue: *Spanish in the United States*).

Joiner, C. 1981. [1979.] Memorandum opinion and order. Civil Action No. 7-71861 (473 F. Supp. 1371). In *Black English and the Education of Children and Youth,* edited by Geneva Smitherman, 336-58. Detroit: Center for Black Studies.

―――. 1978. Order. (451 F. Supp. 1324 and 463 F. Supp. 1027).

Kloss, H. 1977. *The American Bilingual Tradition.* Rowley: Newbury House.

Landers, S. 1989. "English-Only Debate Asks: Is It Polarizing or Uniting?" *Monitor* (January): 26.

Language Policy Committee, Conference on College Composition and Communication. 1987. *Interim Report #1.* 19 October.

Lewis, N. 1989. "Purging 'what-cha' and 'ain't.'" *New York Times.* 28 February.

MacKaye, S. 1988. "California Proposition 63 and Public Perceptions of Language." Paper to be published in Stanford University publication proceedings of Conference on Language Rights. April 1988.

Schwartz, John. [Michigan State Senator.] 1988. Personal communication. 24 May.

Smitherman, G. 1984. "'If you got religion, show some sign': Toward a Language Policy for the Black Community." Paper presented at the Annual Convention, Howard University Black Communications Conference, Washington, D.C.

————. 1986. "Toward a Language Policy for the Black Community." Paper presented at the Annual Convention, Conference on College Composition and Communication, New Orleans.

————, ed. 1981. *Black English and the Education of Black Children and Youth: Proceedings of the National Invitational Symposium on the King Decision.* Detroit: Center for Black Studies.

Smitherman-Donaldson, G. 1987. "Opinion: Toward a National Public Policy on Language." *College English* 49, no. 1 (January): 29–36.

State of Michigan 83rd Legislature. 1985. Section 1157a, amendment to Act. No. 451 of the Public Acts of 1976.

State of Michigan House of Representatives. 1987. *Journal of the House,* 21 October, 2754–55.

State of New Mexico 39th Legislature. 1989. House Joint Memorial 16.

Veltman, C. 1988. *The Future of the Spanish Language in the United States.* New York and Washington, D.C.: Hispanic Policy Development Project.

Woodson, C. G. 1933. *Mis-education of the Negro.* Washington, D.C.: Associated Publishers.

Zentella, A. C. 1988. "Language Politics in the U.S.A.: The English-Only Movement." In *Literature, Language, and Politics,* edited by B. Craige, 39–53. Athens: University of Georgia Press.

12 What One Teacher Can Do

Harvey A. Daniels
National-Louis University

No profession is more profoundly affected by the official-English movement than teaching. For those of us who work in classrooms, and especially we who teach English, laws which change the legal status or public perception of the languages used by our students can dramatically affect our lives. In the educational parlance of the day, English-only makes teachers an "at-risk population." This is why so many of the groups which joined to form the English Plus coalition are teacher associations and why organizations like the National Education Association and the National Council of Teachers of English have taken such strong stands against language protectionism.

But national political action is only one step in fighting linguistic intolerance: other important actions must happen between individual people in our schools and communities. Americans must help each other reconnect with our multilingual heritage—not just to return to the days when language differences were better tolerated, but to move on to an era when plural language abilities are treasured and nurtured as a resource to America. As several authors in this book have shown, the command of multiple languages enriches the intellect and broadens the cultural range of individuals, while it strengthens the country economically, politically, and socially.

Before we recommend steps for individual teachers to take, we must recognize that even educators are not unanimous on this issue. We cannot and do not assume that all teachers are ready to follow the lead of the professional organizations fighting English-only. Though their numbers are relatively small, some teachers are members of U.S. English and are actively working on the other side. For these teachers, just as for other citizens, the drive to officialize the common language apparently seems like either a cautionary message to contemporary immigrants or a patriotic, ceremonial gesture. Still other teachers are caught in the middle, undecided and inactive, feeling torn between the

121

enunciated pluralistic position of their profession and their own worries.

We can only hope that this book, along with other materials and experiences, will help to unify the nation's nearly three million teachers. As educators, we are still heard with a great deal of attention and respect. Though our profession has been besmirched during recent school reform debates, Americans still give special attention to the views of teachers on issues of language and learning. And even more powerfully, citizens and parents in local communities listen intently to individual teachers they know and trust, teachers who have taught their own children, teachers who have proven by their service to the families of a community that they know what is good for kids.

So what can a teacher do to nurture pluralistic language attitudes and practices in his or her own sphere? Following are some possibilities.

Educate Yourself

The English-only movement operates upon staggeringly inaccurate notions of how languages are learned and used. An important start toward critiquing the opposition's arguments—in your own mind and in conversation with others—is to study and internalize the more reliable, coherent models of language developed by linguists. Of course, most of us had a taste of these ideas during our professional training, but for a majority this part of our own education was probably weak and sketchy. Even for teachers of the English language arts, our preparation mainly involved literature and pedagogy, and what we did learn about language itself was most often prescriptive grammar rather than the kind of descriptive sociolinguistics relevant to the official-English controversy.

How can you freshen and deepen your own knowledge of language? Obviously, personal reading is the quickest, simplest, and most individualized way to begin. The reading list at the end of this chapter recommends about twenty books that provide basic background on current linguistic theories, the history of language controversies, treatments of immigration that bear on language panics, and works on bilingual education. A person who reads several of these books will be better prepared to analyze and counter the arguments of English-only advocates.

While there is little treatment of language issues in the general teacher journals and magazines (even the NCTE's offerings for English/language arts teachers cover language issues only rarely), there are a number of more specialized scholarly publications that do address these questions: *Language in Society,* the *International Journal of the Sociology of Language, American Speech, TESOL Quarterly,* and *Written Communication.* The journals serving teachers in ESL and bilingual education programs are another rich source of information.

You might also consider taking a course or two in linguistics— perhaps as an elective in your own ongoing graduate study program. Any course in the history of English, psycholinguistics, child language development, sociolinguistics, dialectology, or applied linguistics would likely be both interesting and helpful. If time, distance, or cost prohibit your taking courses, you could visit your nearest college bookstore, purchase the textbooks for one of these classes, and conduct a do-it-yourself linguistics course. A couple of the more popular texts for introductory linguistics courses are quite suitable for self-study: Fromkin and Rodman's *Language: An Introduction* (Holt, Rinehart and Winston, 1986) and Finegan and Besnier's *Language: Its Structure and Use* (Harcourt, 1989) are two good examples. If you plan to study any of these materials, you might recruit a small group of interested colleagues and form a weekly discussion group to respond to the readings, share experiences, and support each other. If language differences are an issue in your own school or district, perhaps you could request school time and resources for your studies and in return present a teachers' workshop that would educate others.

Show Students Your Own Delight in Diversity

Social change always works better when you begin at a level where you have control, where success depends pretty much on your own efforts. While some of the ideas further down this list require the cooperation of others, we can all begin with what happens when we close our classroom doors.

The most fundamental and powerful message we can send to students, of course, is simply what we are as people, how we feel and act toward language differences. If we really are tolerant, open-minded, curious, even enthusiastic about linguistic and cultural variety, this attitude will transmit itself to students without much conscious effort on our part. At the same time, any confusion, ambivalence, or negativity will also communicate itself—and perhaps that is why we need to be always working on our own education as well.

If you have students from multiple linguistic backgrounds in your classroom, you have a wonderful and automatic opportunity to model a pluralistic outlook in the way you treat students and talk with them.

Beyond routine interaction, a diverse class offers numerous opportunities for the group to talk together about their different languages, to share stories and traditions, to learn bits of each other's tongues.

Teach about Language and Language Differences

The public school curriculum at all levels mandates huge chunks of time for studying language—usually meaning prescriptive rules of grammar, punctuation, and spelling. But you can use some of this time to teach about language descriptively, historically, socially, dynamically. Obviously, the most straightforward way to implement this recommendation is to replace conventional grammar instruction with an age-appropriate version of linguistics. This would be a definite improvement over the traditional curriculum, at least in terms of accuracy and usefulness. For high school classes, an interesting and involving unit on historical linguistics could be built around the excellent PBS series "The Story of English" and its accompanying book. If done with lots of concrete applications and lively projects, this could be a successful experience for older students. But still, replacing traditional grammar study with contemporary linguistics will not necessarily be galvanizing to students.

It's important to study language issues in the context in which they arise—amid social, political, geographical events. But this isn't as hard as it seems. Real linguistics can be taught at any grade level, integrated across the curriculum. For example, when elementary teachers introduce the geography of other states and nations, they can take time to introduce the dialects or languages of those areas, have students sample and discuss these tongues and make comparisons with other languages they know. When students begin reading a book about another region, country, or period—from *Coyote Dreams* to *Huckleberry Finn* to *A Tale of Two Cities*—the teacher can focus students' attention on the language of the author, the time, and place, as part of the experience of the work. Teachers can invite parents who speak other languages to visit the classroom to tell about their home country, to read or tell a traditional story, and to discuss its meaning with the students—with or without help from a translator, as appropriate. When teachers ask students to do research on family or community history, language can play a central role in the resulting reports. Indeed, enterprising English or social studies teachers can help students do linguistic field work, collecting information about languages in the community, interviewing a variety of speakers, conducting usage studies, or sampling linguistic attitudes. Students could even run a questionnaire about neighborhood support for English-only versus English Plus!

Support Second-Language Instruction in Your School

At the heart of English Plus is the belief that bilingualism is better than monolingualism, that people are more fully educated, enriched, and developed when they control multiple communicative systems and can participate in the different cultures those systems carry. This means that we must be just as passionate about native-born monolingual English-speaking children acquiring another language as we are about Hispanic or Asian immigrants learning English. As a school teacher, you can express this concern through support of foreign language programs at all grade levels from elementary school upward, for mixing language groups of students in a variety of instructionally beneficial ways, and for conducting strong bilingual programs for children of limited-English proficiency. You can support these activities simply by speaking out as a concerned colleague and staff member but also, when the opportunity arises, through participation on curriculum committees, planning groups, accreditation reviews, and other formal mechanisms of school policy development.

Work to Reform Your School's Curriculum along Multi-ethnic, Multilingual Lines

By the middle of the next century, those peoples whom we now call ethnic minorities will be the numerical majority of United States residents. We are moving toward a culturally diverse, complex, and rich future which most school curricula do not yet reflect, or even accept. You can provide a great service to the students, parents, and faculty of your own school community by helping people review the curriculum in light of the new multicultural realities of your own part of America. In practice, this may mean calling for (and volunteering to serve on) a new curriculum review council or task force, or assisting in the work of some ongoing body.

Many of the issues that need to be considered will concern specific courses and materials, such as the treatment of different groups in social studies and history books, the range of literature used in English classes, the nature of assistance to limited-English-proficient students, and the availability of second-language learning opportunities for monolingual children. But also of concern may be deeper institutional issues, such as ability-grouping or "tracking" practices which segregate students by language and ethnicity; representation of ethnic and linguistic minorities on the faculty; and relationships between the school and different groups in the community.

Join English Plus

There is an organized national movement for linguistic pluralism and against protectionism. It is called English Plus, and anyone can join by writing the EPIC office in Washington, D. C. Originally founded in 1987 as a coalition of 30 concerned groups, EPIC enunciates its purposes as follows:

> The core of the strength and vitality of the United States is the diversity of our people, and our constitutional commitment to equal protection under the law. Now, more than ever, our commitment to cultural and democratic pluralism is essential to enhance our competitiveness and position of international leadership. In an interdependent world, the diversity of our people provides a unique reservoir of understanding.
>
> The "English Plus" concept holds that the national interest can best be served when all members of our society have full access to effective opportunities to acquire strong English-language proficiency plus mastery of a second or multiple languages. "English Plus" holds that there is a need for a vastly expanded network of facilities and programs for comprehensive instruction in English and other languages. "English Plus" rejects the ideology and divisive character of the so-called "English-only" movement. "English Plus" holds that national unity and our constitutional values require that language assistance be made available in order to ensure equal access to essential services, education, the electoral process, and other rights and opportunities guaranteed to all members of society. (*EPIC Events*, 1988, March/April, 2)

If these statements reflect your views, join up. For a basic membership fee of $18.00, you will receive the informative *EPIC Events* newsletter. Any greater amount serves as a tax-deductible donation to EPIC's work. Make your check payable to the National Forum (EPIC's fiscal agent) and send it to 200 I Street, Washington, D.C. 20002. Please designate EPIC on your check.

Become Active in Your Local and National Professional Societies

Most teachers can choose to join a variety of professional groups, depending upon their classroom assignment and teaching specialty. Among these are The National Council of Teachers of English, The National Association for Bilingual Education, and many others. Membership in any of these groups can help you stay abreast of contemporary instructional issues and research, and will often provide, through their journals or book offerings, information about language politics.

These associations also need active members who can help them monitor and act upon language protection issues. So, you should propose presentations for local and national conventions that focus on English-only/English Plus. Enlist colleagues concerned with these matters to join you on the podium. Write and submit articles for both local and regional newsletters, as well as state and national journals. When there are chances to form committees, develop documents, or plan events, volunteer to take a leading role.

Work for Proactive Legislation in Your Community or State

Though U.S. English has garnered more publicity for its statewide English-only referenda, many municipalities have passed resolutions officially celebrating their multilingualism and multi-ethnicity. Among these have been Denver, Atlanta, Cleveland, Dallas, the District of Columbia, San Antonio, and Tucson, as well as many smaller communities. The proclamation of Osceola County, Florida, for example, offers an inspiring and easily-revised model for other localities:

Osceola County, Florida
August 4, 1986

Whereas, it is the welcome responsibility of Osceola County to respect the efforts of all cultural, ethnic and linguistic segments of the population in their desire to enter the mainstream of American life; and

Whereas, the history of Osceola County has been beneficially and inextricably interlaced with that of its large and growing multicultural population, and

Whereas, the diverse ethnic and linguistic communities have enriched the quality of life in Osceola County and have contributed directly to its prosperity; and

Whereas, Osceola County is a financial and cultural center of the Southeast development, international commerce, banking, tourism and foreign investment through the diversity of its population; and

Whereas, Osceola County is committed to the principles of diversity and pluralism and encourages its ethnic communities to honor the cultural and linguistic heritages of their respective lands of origin.

Now Therefore Be It Resolved By the Osceola County Commissioners, that the County of Osceola is designated as multicultural, multilingual, and that the respect for all languages and cultures is integral to its continued prosperity. (*EPIC Events*, 1988, September/October, 8)

If the time seems right for your town, country, or state, and you have the energy and ambition, you might form a group of colleagues and friends to begin the legwork necessary to pass such legislation.

Fight the English-Only Movement

Write your senators and congresspersons and let them know your views, as a teacher and citizen. Tell them to keep the ELA bottled up in committee, where it belongs—or to vote it down if it ever gets out. If your state is targeted in the next round of official-English referenda initiatives, help organize the opposition. Form your own local chapter of English Plus, gather colleagues and friends, and campaign. Often, teachers can be especially helpful by writing position papers or serving as spokespeople. Arizona's 1988 initiative only passed by 51 percent. Now that its immigration restriction roots are starting to circulate, U.S. English is vulnerable to an embarrassing defeat. You could help it happen in your state.

Recommended Readings on Language Protection Issues

Abrahams, Roger D., and Rudolph C. Troike. 1972. *Language and Cultural Diversity in American Education*. Englewood Cliffs, N.J.: Prentice-Hall.

Baron, Dennis. Forthcoming. *The English-Only Question: An Official Language for Americans?*

———. 1982. *Grammar and Good Taste: Reforming American Language*. New Haven: Yale University Press.

Butler, Melvin A., Chair, and the Committee on CCCC Language Statement. 1974. "Students' Right to Their Own Language." Special Issue of *College Composition and Communication* 25(Fall): 1–32.

Chase, Allan. 1977. *The Legacy of Malthus: The Social Costs of the New Scientific Racism.* New York: Alfred A. Knopf.

Clark, Virginia P., Paul A. Eschholz, and Alfred F. Rosa. 1987. *Language: Introductory Readings.* New York: St. Martins Press.

Crawford, James. 1989. *Bilingual Education: History, Politics, Theory and Practice.* Trenton, New Jersey: Crane Publishing Company.

Daniels, Harvey A. 1983. *Famous Last Words: The American Language Crisis Reconsidered.* Carbondale: Southern Illinois University Press.

EPIC Events (Newsletter of the English Plus Information Clearinghouse). 1988. Washington, D.C.: March/April, September/October.

Farr, Marcia, and Harvey Daniels. 1988. *Language Diversity and Writing Instruction.* Urbana: NCTE.

Ferguson, Charles A., and Shirley Brice Heath, eds. 1981. *Language in the USA.* Cambridge, Mass.: Cambridge University Press.

Finegan, Edward. 1980. *Attitudes toward English Usage: History of a War of Words.* New York: Teachers College Press.

Fishman, Joshua, ed. 1978. *Language Loyalty in the United States: The Maintenance and Perpetuation of Non-English Mother Tongues by American Ethnic and Religious Groups.* New York: Arno Press.

Gere, Anne Ruggles, and Eugene Smith. 1979. *Language, Attitudes, and Change.* Urbana: National Council of Teachers of English.

Gould, Steven Jay. 1981. *The Mismeasure of Man.* New York: W. W. Norton.

Hakuta, Kenji. 1986. *The Mirror of Language: The Debate on Bilingualism.* New York: Basic Books.

Heath, Shirley Brice. 1983. *Ways with Words, Language, Life, and Work in Communities and Classrooms.* Cambridge, Mass.: Cambridge University Press.

Higham, John. 1963. *Strangers in the Land: Patterns of American Nativism 1860–1925.* New York: Atheneum.

McDavid, Raven I., ed. 1971. *An Investigation of the Attitudes of the NCTE toward Usage.* Urbana: National Council of Teachers of English.

Marshall, David F. 1986. "The Question of an Official Language: Language Rights and the English Language Amendment." Special issue of the *International Journal of the Sociology of Language.* The Hague: Mouton.

Quinn, Jim. 1980. *American Tongue and Cheek: A Populist Guide to our Language.* New York: Pantheon.

Editor

Harvey A. Daniels is professor of education and chair of the Department of Interdisciplinary Studies at National-Louis University in Evanston, Illinois. Daniels is the author or coauthor of four other books on language and education, including *Famous Last Words: The American Language Crisis Reconsidered* (Southern Illinois University Press, 1983) and *Language Diversity and Writing Instruction* (NCTE, 1986). Daniels served as a member of the NCTE's Commission on Language from 1986 to 1989, a time when the Council officially condemned the English-only movement. This volume grew out of the Commission's desire to have the NCTE's position on language restrictionism more fully explained and widely disseminated.

Contributors

Dennis Baron is professor of English and linguistics and director of rhetoric at the University of Illinois at Urbana-Champaign. He edits the monograph series, *Publication of the American Dialect Society* and has served on NCTE's Commission on the English Language. He is the author of *Grammar and Good Taste: Reforming the American Language* (Yale, 1982), *Grammar and Gender* (Yale, 1986), and *Declining Grammar* (NCTE, 1989), and is a regular language commentator for WILL-AM in Urbana. In 1989 he held a National Endowment for the Humanities Fellowship while working on his next book, *The English-Only Question: An Official Language for Americans?*

Mary Carol Combs is the former director of the English Plus Information Clearinghouse (EPIC) in Washington, D.C., where she coordinated efforts to research language rights and public policy issues in the United States. In addition to articles and opinion editorials about the discriminary nature of the English-only movement, she edited *EPIC Events*, a national newsletter about language and language policy issues. Currently, she is pursuing a Ph.D. in multicultural education at the University of Arizona in Tucson.

Vivian I. Davis teaches developmental writing and freshman composition in the Division of Communications and Developmental Studies at Eastfield College in Mesquite, Texas, where her classes are comprised of students from a diversity of racial and ethnic backgrounds. She was formerly chair of the English Department at Parrent County Junior College in Fort Worth, Texas, and she has taught English at the high school level, as well as at the two-year college and four-year college levels, both to undergraduate and graduate students. She has also been active in teacher training. A long-time member of NCTE, Professor Davis is the author of numerous professional articles.

Elizabeth Frick is project manager for adult literacy and work readiness products for Applied Learning, the largest training company in the world. Frick has taught English and communications in elementary school, middle school, high school, and college, as well as in state correctional institutions. In addition to publishing in sociolinguistic journals, Frick recently edited *Synthesis: Becoming Technical Instructors*, a handbook for 3M's technical instructors. She has also conducted technical training workshops for 3M and edited several publications for 3M's human resources and technical education. Frick also has several years of consulting experience with First Bank, Control Data, West Publishing, Century 21, U.S. Fish and Wildlife, and the University Research Consortium.

Roseann Dueñas Gonzalez is associate professor of English at the University of Arizona. She also directs the English as a second language graduate program and the writing skills improvement program there. She has published a number of articles, monographs, and textbooks on English as a second language, minority education, language policy, and other language-related issues. She has served as chair of the NCTE Task Force on Racism and Bias in the Teaching of English, and she is currently cochair of the NCTE Hispanic Caucus, as well as a member of the executive board of the NCTE ESL Assembly. She has served the Council in numerous capacities over the past 18 years.

Elliot L. Judd is assistant professor of linguistics and the director of the TESOL program at the University of Illinois at Chicago. He has previously taught at The Univerisad Central de Venezuela (as a Senior Fulbright lecturer), Ohio University, SUNY-Cortland, and in several adult ESL programs in the New York City area. He is coeditor of *Sociolinguistics and Language Acquisition* and *On TESOL '84*. He has also published numerous journal articles and book chapters on language and politics, ESL/EFL methodology, and teacher training. He is currently the chair of the TOEFL Committee of Examiners and has held several positions in the TESOL association.

Lynn M. Lynch is a freelance writer specializing in language-related topics. She holds a B.A. in English from Kenyon College and an M.S. in applied linguistics from Georgetown University. In addition to teaching English as a foreign language in Buenos Aires, Argentina, she has served as a writer and editorial consultant for numerous firms, including Time-Life Books, Rodale Press, and the American Horticultural Society. Her articles have appeared in *English Today, Irish America Magazine,* and *American Horticulturist,* among others. Ms. Lynch currently resides in Mifflinburg, Pennsylvania.

James Sledd, "President-for-Life" of the "Whole Child Foundation," is professor emeritus at the University of Texas at Austin. In his own words, "he has written and talked a great deal more than he should have, but is consoled for his antiquity by the knowledge that the Respectable consider him a Trouble-Maker."

Geneva Smitherman is professor and director of the African-American language and literacy program in the Department of English at Michigan State University. She chairs the Language Policy Committee of the Conference on College Composition and Communication, and she is chief editor of the African-American Life series at Wayne State University Press. An internationally recognized authority on Black English, Smitherman is author of *Talkin' and Testifyin': The Language of Black America* and of over 50 articles in the area of language variation and African-American studies. She is also coeditor, with Teun A. van Dijk, of *Discourse and Discrimination.* She began her career as a Detroit high school teacher of English and Latin, and she has held faculty positions at the University of Michigan, Harvard University, Wayne State University, and this past summer at Oxford University. Recipient of a recent NCTE Research Foundation grant to study African-

American essays in the National Assessment of Educational Progress, Smitherman has served on the NCTE Commission on Language, the Modern Language Association's Commission on Minorities, and the board of *American Speech*. Currently, she is on the editorial boards of *College Composition and Communication, Howard Journal of Communication,* and *Urban Educator,* and she is an associate editor of the new MLA book series, *Research and Scholarship in Composition*. She has frequently been called upon for expert opinion by the broadcast media and the courts. Smitherman's awards and honors include the Educational Press Association Award for Excellence in Journalism and the Outstanding Woman of the Year Award from the National Association of Negro Business and Professional Women's Young Adult Club.

James C. Stalker is a professor of English linguistics at Michigan State University where he also directs the intensive English program and the master's TESOL program. His current research focus is on the discourse structure and pragmatic functions of standard English and other varieties of English. Professor Stalker continues a long-term interest in stylistics, particularly in the structure and function of the poetic line.

Victor Villanueva, Jr., is assistant professor of rhetoric and composition theory at Northern Arizona University. A latecomer to academics, having returned to school to complete high school after attempting a career in the military, receiving a Ph.D. from a major university a decade later, his research and publications focus on the kinds of political and psychological constraints which are imposed on minorities. He has directed an educational opportunity program aimed at minorities and economically disadvantaged nonminority students and has directed a major writing project site. He has served on various NCTE committees, including the Commission on Language, and is the present chair of the NCTE Committee on Racism and Bias in the Teaching of English.